pinpoint
ENGLISH
comprehension

Y4

Published by Pearson Education Limited, 80 Strand, London, WC2R 0RL.

www.pearsonschools.co.uk

This edition is published by arrangement with Teacher Created Materials, Inc. for sale throughout the world.

Text © Pearson Education Limited 2018
Questions authored by Lindsay Pickton and Christine Chen
Designed by Pearson Education Limited 2018
Typeset by PDQ Digital Media Solutions Ltd.
Original illustrations © Pearson Education Limited 2018
Cover design and illustration by Eva Caldas

First published 2018

21 20 19 18
10 9 8 7 6 5 4 3 2 1

British Library Cataloguing in Publication Data
A catalogue record for this book is available from the British Library

ISBN 978 1 292 26686 2

Copyright notice
All rights reserved. The material in this publication is copyright. Activity sheets may be freely photocopied for classroom use in the purchasing institution. However, this material is copyright and under no circumstances may copies be offered for sale. If you wish to use the material in any way other than that specified you must apply in writing to the publishers.

Printed in the UK by Ashford Press Ltd

Acknowledgements
Text credits
p55: Text Copyright © 2007 David Almond My Dad's A Birdman by David Almond & illustrated by Polly Dunbar. Reproduced by permission of Walker Books Ltd, London SE11 5HJ www.walker.co.uk; **p16**: School Tomorrow - Excuses for Mum by Joseph Cohelo published by Frances Lincoln Ltd, copyright © 2014. Reproduced by permission of Frances Lincoln Ltd, an imprint of The Quarto Group; **p31**: Holland, Kevin Crossley, Heartsong, © 2015, first published in the UK by Orchard Books, an imprint of Hachette Children's Books, Carmelite House, 50 Victoria Embankment, London, EC4Y 0DZ, and reproduced by permission; **p51**: I Like to Stay Up © Grace Nichols, 1984. Reproduced with permission of Curtis Brown Group Ltd, London, on behalf of Grace Nichols.

Photographs
(Key: T-top; B-bottom; C-centre; L-left; R-right)
Shutterstock: Mikael Damkier 12b, Sari ONeal 27cr, Everett Historical 7b, AdamEdwards 76b, my-summit 91b, **Alamy Stock Photo**: Cultural Archive 67br, **Pearson India Education Services Pvt. Ltd**: Mohd Suhail 37.

Note from the publisher
Pearson has robust editorial processes, including answer and fact checks, to ensure the accuracy of the content in this publication, and every effort is made to ensure this publication is free of errors. We are, however, only human, and occasionally errors do occur. Pearson is not liable for any misunderstandings that arise as a result of errors in this publication, but it is our priority to ensure that the content is accurate. If you spot an error, please do contact us at resourcescorrections@pearson.com so we can make sure it is corrected.

Contents

Year 4

How does it work?		4
Unit 1	**Non-fiction:** The Life of Amelia Earhart	6
Unit 2	**Non-fiction:** Hitting the Slopes	11
Unit 3	**Poetry:** School Tomorrow – Excuses for Mum by Joseph Coelho	16
Unit 4	**Classic fiction:** The Jungle Book by Rudyard Kipling	21
Unit 5	**Non-fiction:** Monarch Butterflies	26
Unit 6	**Fiction:** Heartsong by Kevin Crossley-Holland	31
Unit 7	**Non-fiction:** Stargazing	36
Unit 8	**Classic fiction:** Alice's Adventures in Wonderland by Lewis Carroll	41
Unit 9	**Fiction:** Taking the Shot	46
Unit 10	**Poetry:** I Like to Stay Up by Grace Nichols	51
Unit 11	**Fiction:** My Dad's a Birdman by David Almond	55
Unit 12	**Classic fiction:** The Merry Adventures of Robin Hood by Howard Pyle	61
Unit 13	**Non-fiction:** Natural Measures	66
Unit 14	**Fiction:** My Lemonade Stand	71
Unit 15	**Non-fiction:** Sleeping for Survival	76
Unit 16	**Classic fiction:** The Secret Garden by Frances Hodgson Burnett	81
Unit 17	**Poetry:** Who Has Seen the Wind? and Hurt No Living Thing by Christina Rossetti	86
Unit 18	**Non-fiction:** Mount Everest	90
Unit 19	**Non-fiction:** Making Room for Bikes	95
Unit 20	**Fiction:** The Lion's Share	99
Answers		104

Year 4

How does it work?

Pinpoint English Comprehension provides targeted practice of a wide range of comprehension strategies, including higher-order skills. The series has been carefully written to ensure children encounter varied question types to mirror the demands of the Key Stage 2 National Curriculum tests. Each unit follows a familiar, scaffolded structure so that all children can feel comfortable working independently.

The units use a variety of text types including poetry, classic and contemporary fiction, and stimulating non-fiction. Each unit features one text with comprehension questions organised into three levels:

These questions are a necessary step towards age-related expectations.
Towards is largely comprised of selected response or short constructed response questions to develop retrieval skills and encourage careful reading. However, to ensure children experience a variety of question types, **Towards** also includes vocabulary questions, simple inference questions and occasional extended response questions.

These questions are pitched at age-related expectations.
Securing includes a wide range of comprehension question types in the form of selected response and short and extended constructed response questions to help in the development of comprehension strategies, including higher-order skills.

These questions challenge children to tackle complex questions requiring a broad range of comprehension strategies, especially those higher-order skills such as inference. Short constructed response and complex selected response questions are also included to ensure children experience a variety of question types at greater depth. At this stage, children are more frequently required to explain their thinking, with evidence.

The resources are **designed to be used flexibly**. Select *Towards*, *Securing* or *Deeper*, as appropriate depending on the level your children are working at. Each of the three sets of questions is unique; there is no repetition between Towards, Securing and Deeper, so children can complete one, two or even all three sets of questions in each unit.

Year 4

Pinpoint English Comprehension and the National Curriculum

The content and cognitive domains

All questions have been written to support the Key Stage 2 content and cognitive domains which set out the comprehension elements of the National Curriculum and are the basis of National Curriculum test questions. The table below shows the content domains.

Content domain references (from Key Stage 2 English reading test framework)	
2a	give / explain the meaning of words in context
2b	retrieve and record information / identify key details from fiction and non-fiction
2c	summarise main ideas from more than one paragraph
2d	make inferences from the text / explain and justify inferences with evidence from the text
2e	predict what might happen from details stated and implied
2f	identify / explain how information / content is related & contributes to meaning as a whole
2g	identify / explain how meaning is enhanced through choice of words and phrases
2h	make comparisons within the text

You can find the content domain references in the answer mark scheme on pages 104 to 143.

Comprehension strategies

Questions have also been written to cover the following comprehension strategies, based on the *Reading – Comprehension* section of the National Curriculum English Programme of Study (Years 5 and 6):

- Retrieving and recording information
- Recall
- Making inferences
- Clarifying
- Summarising
- Visualising
- Making connections
- Evaluating
- Making comparisons within the text
- Giving meaning of words in context
- Identifying / explaining how meaning is enhanced
- Empathising

You can find information about question-by-question coverage of comprehension strategies in the answer mark scheme on pages 104 to 143.

Pinpoint English Comprehension can help teachers to deliver:

- **Scottish Curriculum for Excellence:** literacy and English experiences and outcomes for Reading at Second Level
- **Programme of Study for English in Wales at Key Stage 2:** Comprehension aspect of the Reading Strand
- **Northern Ireland Curriculum:** Statutory Requirements for Literacy and Language at Key Stage 2 (Reading)

Answer mark scheme

There are detailed answers on pages 104 to 143 which reflect the National Curriculum reading test mark scheme. For each question, you will find acceptable answers together with details about the content domain, comprehension strategies and mark allocation. In addition, the mark scheme provides helpful notes and guidance about commonly made mistakes.

Unit 1

The Life of Amelia Earhart

Amelia Earhart was born in the United States of America (USA) in 1897. She was always an adventurous child. She had lots of ambitious ideas about what to do when she grew up. But she never thought of becoming a pilot. When she was about 20 years old, she rode as a passenger in a plane. It changed her life. She was instantly hooked on flying.

Earhart took her first flying lesson in 1921. She worked hard to save up money to buy a plane. First she worked as a nursing assistant and then as a social worker. When she had enough money, she bought a bright yellow plane. She called it *Canary*.

> *Altitude* means how high up in the air something is.

Earhart learned a lot about flying in *Canary*. She flew to an altitude of 4,270 metres. That was a record at that time. Her next record was being the first woman to cross the Atlantic Ocean in a plane. That time, she was not allowed to pilot the plane. She was just a passenger, while two men took the controls.

Soon, being a passenger was not enough for Earhart. She wanted to fly a plane across the Atlantic herself, and she wanted to do it alone. After careful planning, in 1932 she set off from Canada to make her solo flight across the Atlantic to France. Bad weather forced her to land in Ireland, but it was still a great achievement. She had shown the world that a woman could fly a plane solo across the Atlantic.

On 12th January, 1935, Earhart went on to complete a solo flight across 2,300 miles (3,700 kilometres) of the Pacific Ocean, from Honolulu to California.

Flying Fact!
During her solo flight across the Pacific, Amelia often enjoyed a cup of hot chocolate!

Next, Amelia Earhart set out to tackle another challenge. She wanted to be the first woman to fly around the world. She and her co-pilot, Fred Noonan, left the USA on 1st June 1937 in a specially-built plane, the *Electra*. They travelled over 20,000 miles (32,187 kilometres). By 2nd July, the trip was almost complete. The *Electra* took off from New Guinea, an island north of Australia, in poor weather. Earhart had difficulty hearing messages through her radio. She reported that she was 'running north and south'. Then the line went silent. Those were the last words anyone ever heard from her. Experts are still trying to solve the mystery of what happened to Amelia Earhart, Fred Noonan and the *Electra*.

Amelia Earhart's achievements and bravery are still inspiring today.

Unit 1

Name _____

Class _____

1 Mark the statements about Amelia Earhart as a child as true or false. The first one has been done for you. [2]

	True	False
She wanted to become a pilot.		✓
She was ambitious.	✓	
She wanted to fly across the Atlantic.		✓
She was adventurous.	✓	

2 Draw lines to match the years to the facts about Amelia Earhart. The first one has been done for you. [2]

Years	What happened to Amelia Earhart
1897	first solo flight across the Atlantic
1921	first flying lesson
1932	flew across the Pacific
1935	was born
1937	left the USA in the *Electra*

3 **Find** and **copy one** word in the *Flying Fact!* section that tells you Amelia flew *alone*. [1]

> Swap *alone* for other words and check the sentence still makes sense.

_____

4 What were the **two** jobs that Amelia Earhart did to help her save up for her first plane? [2]

1. _____

2. _____

> Scan the text for where it says *she worked as…*

Name _____

Class _____

Unit 1

1 Number the list of events from Amelia Earhart's life 1-5 to put them in the right order. The first one has been done for you. [1]

She flew from Canada to Ireland. ☐

She had flying lessons. ☐ 1

She set off in the *Electra* to fly around the world. ☐

She flew across the Pacific Ocean alone. ☐

She became the first woman to cross the Atlantic in a plane. ☐

2 '*She was instantly hooked on flying.*'
What does *instantly hooked* tell you about her attitude to flying? Tick **one** box. [1]

immediately gripped ☐   totally ambitious ☐

a little bit curious ☐   trained straight away ☐

3 According to the text, what **two** records did Amelia Earhart break before 1932? [2]

Read the question carefully!

1. _____

2. _____

4 '*Next, Amelia Earhart set out to tackle another challenge.*'
Which of the below best matches the meaning of *tackle*? [1]

dodge away from ☐   cuddle up to ☐

fight hard ☐   get to grips with ☐

© Pearson Education Limited 2018   *Pinpoint English Comprehension Year 4*

Unit 1

Name _____

Class _____

1 In this text, two of Amelia Earhart's planes are named: one is her first plane, and one is her last. Finish these sentences by adding in the names, and explaining how you know which is which. [2]

I know the _____ was her first plane because _____ .

I know the _____ was her last plane because _____ .

2 What problems and obstacles did Amelia Earhart face as a pilot? Use the whole text to give **three** examples. [3]

> Look for the problems she had – they are quite different from one another.

1. _____

2. _____

3. _____

3 Find examples from throughout Amelia Earhart's life of her independence and determination. [3]

_____

_____

_____

3 'Experts are still trying to solve the mystery …'
Why is it still a *mystery*? [1]

_____

_____

10 © Pearson Education Limited 2018 Pinpoint English Comprehension Year 4

Unit 2

Hitting the Slopes

Snowboarding or skiing

At any ski centre around the world you can see skiers and snowboarders on the slopes together. These two sports did not always share slope space so happily. It took a while for people to accept snowboarding. Today, it is one of the most popular winter sports.

> **Fun Fact!**
> The word *snurf* is a cross between the words *snow* and *surf*.

Skiing involves gliding down snowy hills with a ski (a long strip of plastic) under each foot. Skiers hold a stick in each hand, which they use to help them balance and to push themselves forwards.

Snowboarding is riding over the snow while standing on a flat board. Snowboarders wear special boots which are strapped to their snowboard.

Experienced skiers and snowboarders can do tricks, jumps and spins.

When did snowboarding start?

Many people think that snowboarding is a recent sport. In fact, snowboarding probably started in the 1920s. People rode on a piece of wood which they tied to their feet with horse reins. In 1965, one skier had a unique idea. He tied two skis together and put a rope at the front to steer it. The skier called this a snurfer.

The idea of snurfing took off and people started to make new kinds of snurfers for snurfing competitions. In the 1970s, people started to experiment with the design of the board, adding flexible straps for the feet, which made it possible to do jumps and tricks. The design developed further throughout the 1980s. Eventually it became the snowboard we know today.

> **Fun Fact!**
> The length of a snowboard depends on the height of the user. Most people use a board that would come up to their chin, but in snowboarding competitions, they use snowboards that stand tall above your head!

Unit 2
Hitting the Slopes

How did snowboarding become popular?

More and more people became interested in snowboarding, but it was hard to find places to practise as some slopes only allowed skiers. They worried that snowboards would sweep the snow off the mountain and spoil the ski runs, but attitudes gradually began to change.

Snowboarding became an Olympic sport in 1998. It gained popularity as snowboarders showed off their amazing skills. People were captivated, and many wanted to have a go for themselves. Before long, snowboarding was as common as skiing.

A ski run is a path down a mountain for snow skiing.

Snowboarding as a spectator sport

Fans like to watch snowboarding competitions on the slopes or on television. Many people enjoy seeing the top athletes performing in a half-pipe. Snowboarders ride from one side to the other, jumping and doing breathtaking somersaults and spins inside the half-pipe. It takes a lot of practice to do these tricks, but it is a lot of fun too!

A half-pipe is a U-shaped bowl, similar to the curved slopes used in skateboarding.

Name _____

Class _____

Unit 2

1. According to the text, what can top skiers and snowboarders both do? [1]

   Re-read the end of the first section.

   _____

2. Draw lines to match the equipment to the sport, as described in the text. [1]

Sport	Equipment
skiing	two long plastic strips
	flat board
snowboarding	special boots
	sticks for balance

   Read the section When did snowboarding start? carefully.

3. Give **two** things you can learn about *snurfing* from this text. [2]

   1. _____

   2. _____

4. **Find** and **copy** the **group of words** that tells you more and more people liked the sport of snowboarding. [1]

   _____

5. Mark these facts as true or false. The first one has been done for you. [2]

	True	False
Snowboarding is a recent sport.		✓
Snowboarding was not accepted straightaway.		
Snurfing turned into snowboarding.		
Snurfboards were pulled by horses.		

   © Pearson Education Limited 2018   Pinpoint English Comprehension Year 4

Unit 2

Name _____

Class _____

1 What did people add to their boards to make jumps and tricks possible for snurfers? [1]

_____

2 Mark the statements about the length of snowboards as true or false. The first one has been done for you. [2]

Read the fact box.

	True	False
They are all the same length.		✓
They usually come up to the user's chin.		
They are longer for racers.		
They are different lengths depending on the weight of the user.		

3 'Attitudes gradually began to change …'
What does this tell you about skiers' views on snowboarding? [2]

_____

_____

4 **Find** and **copy one** word that tells you the sport grabbed people's attention. [1]

Try swapping words and making sure the sentence still makes good sense.

_____

Name _____

Class _____

Unit 2

1 Why did few ski centres allow snowboarders on their runs, at first? Identify two reasons by ticking **two** statements below. [2]

☐ They did not have the space for both skiing and boarding.

☐ In case snowboarders ruined their ski runs.

☐ It was dangerous to have both skiiers and boarders on the runs.

☐ They were worried snow would be swept off by the boards.

2 Why are the somersaults and spins of top athletes described as *breathtaking*? [2]

> Try to picture in your mind what it would feel like to watch these stunts!

_____

_____

3 From your reading of the whole text, which of the titles below would make a good alternative to *Hitting the Slopes*? Tick **one** box. [1]

☐ Snowboarding is the Best

☐ The Birth and Growth of Snowboarding

☐ Olympic Snurfing

☐ Battle on the Slopes

4 How has snowboarding changed since the 1920s? Give **three** ways, using evidence from across the text. [3]

1. _____

2. _____

3. _____

Unit 3: School Tomorrow – Excuses for Mum

By Joseph Coelho

Back at school tomorrow.
Not tomorrow!
One more day off please.
I'm sick.
I'm not ready.
I haven't done my homework.

We don't do much the first week back.
Miss won't mind if I miss one day.
My uniform is dirty.
I can't remember where the school is.

I want to stay home with you.
We should spend more quality time together.

I need a few more days to grow up.
I won't know anyone – they'll all be older.
The school fell down during the summer.
The school has flooded.
The school ran away.
The school is still on holiday.

Unit 3

I can't go to school tomorrow …
My foot hurts.
My leg hurts.
My arm hurts.
My face hurts.
My belly hurts.
I have the runs.
I have heat stroke.
I have the plague!

I'll stay home and clean and cook.
I'll pay the bills,
sort out the tax,
handle the builders,
get the shopping.
I won't see my friends.
I'll miss that topic about the Romans.
I won't find out my results.
I won't get to laugh in assembly,
or joke with Mr Lindon.
I won't play football.
I won't make a circuit.
Or get to quote Shakespeare …

Where's my uniform?

Unit 3

Name _____

Class _____

1 Look at the verse which begins, '*I can't go to school tomorrow …*'. What is this verse all about? [1]

_____

2 Mark these statements about the whole poem as true or false. The first one has been done for you [2]

Read the whole poem before answering.

	True	False
At the beginning, the boy can't wait to go to school.		✓
He's talking to his mum.		
He's really, really ill.		
In the end, he really wants to go to school.		

3 **Find** and **copy one** word in the verse beginning *I'll stay home and clean and cook* that means the same as *deal with*. [1]

_____

4 List **three** things the boy realises that he will miss if he doesn't go to school. [3]

The answer is in the last full verse.

1. _____

2. _____

3. _____

© Pearson Education Limited 2018   Pinpoint English Comprehension Year 4

Name _____

Class _____

Unit **3**

1 Draw lines to show which of these excuses that the boy makes are realistic, and which are unrealistic.
The first two have been done for you. [2]

> Read the whole poem before answering.

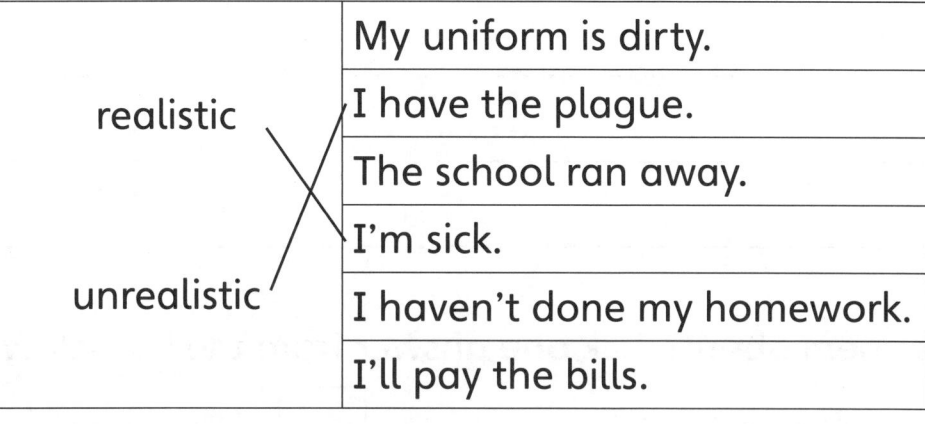

2 *'Not tomorrow!'*
What feeling is the poet suggesting with the use of an exclamation mark here? [1]

_____

3 What is the effect of having so many excuses listed together?
Mark the answers as true or false.
The first one has been done for you. [2]

	True	False
It seems more desperate.	✓	
It makes it sound like a story.		
It makes his change of mind more surprising.		
It is funny and unbelievable.		
It is like a shopping list.		

© Pearson Education Limited 2018 — Pinpoint English Comprehension Year 4

Unit 3 D

Name _____

Class _____

1 In the final verse, what does the boy realise about staying at home? Give **two** things and support your answer with details from the poem. [3]

1. _____
   _____

2. _____
   _____

2 What is this poem about? Tick **one** answer from the list below. [1]

A boy who is not very well. ☐

A boy who realises he likes school. ☐

A boy who wants to stay with his mum. ☐

A boy who hates homework. ☐

> Think about the meaning of the whole poem.

3 Why might this poem be seen as funny by many people? Try to explain in detail. [3]

_____
_____
_____
_____

> Think about which things make you laugh or smile in this poem.

The Jungle Book

An excerpt adapted from the original by Rudyard Kipling.

Rikki-tikki, the mongoose, has been adopted into a British family living in India. The family keep Rikki-tikki as a pet for protection against cobras.

Old books say that when a mongoose fights a snake and gets bitten, he runs off, eats some herbs and it cures him. That is not true. The mongoose survives the snake's attack because of the quickness of his eye and his foot. A snake's head strikes faster than the eye can see, but the mongoose has a jump that is more wonderful than a magical herb. Rikki-tikki was pleased that he had escaped from a cobra's bite with his astonishing jump. It made him proud. When Teddy came running over, Rikki-tikki was ready to be petted.

> A *mongoose* is a wild animal, similar to a wild cat.

But just as Teddy was stooping down to Rikki-tikki, something wriggled in the dust. A tiny voice said, "Be careful. I am Death!" It was a karait, a dusty brown snake that lies on the dusty earth. His bite is as deadly as the cobra's but he is so small that no one thinks of him. So he actually does more harm to people than the cobra.

Rikki-tikki danced up to the karait with the odd rocking, swaying motion that all mongooses have when they walk. It looks funny, but it means they can fly off in any direction. If you have to deal with snakes, this is a good thing. Rikki-tikki did not know that fighting the karait was much more dangerous than fighting the cobra. The karait is small and can turn quickly. Unless Rikki-tikki bit him close to the back of the head, he would get bitten in his eye or his lip. But Rikki-tikki did not know this.

> The cobra and the karait are both types of venomous snake.

Unit 4

The Jungle Book

The karait struck out and Rikki-tikki jumped to the side. Then Rikki-tikki tried to run at the snake, but the karait's wicked little dusty grey head lashed within a fraction of his shoulder. Rikki-tikki had to jump over its body and the snake's head followed his heels closely.

Teddy shouted to the house, "Oh, look here! Our mongoose is killing a snake." Rikki-tikki heard Teddy's mother scream. His father ran out with a stick, but by the time he came up, the karait had lunged out too far. Rikki-tikki had sprung. He jumped on the snake's back and bit as high up its back as he could get hold, then he rolled away. That bite paralysed the karait. Rikki-tikki was about to eat him from the tail up, but then he remembered that a full meal makes a slow mongoose. If he wanted all his strength and quickness, he must stay thin. He went away for a dust bath under the bushes.

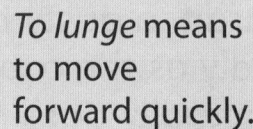

To lunge means to move forward quickly.

Then Teddy's mother picked Rikki-tikki up from the dust. She hugged him and cried that he had saved Teddy from death.

Name _____

Class _____

Unit 4

1 What made Rikki-tikki feel proud? Tick **one** box. [1]

his knowledge of herbs ☐   the snake's speed ☐

his jumping skills ☐   Teddy's running ☐

2 '"*Be careful. I am Death!*"'

Who says this in the story? [1]

_____

Read the first paragraph carefully.

3 Why is the karait a real danger?
Mark the answers true or false.
The first one has been done for you. [2]

	True	False
He can turn quickly.	✓	
His bite is as deadly as a cobra's.		
He has a special swaying motion.		
He can fly off in any direction.		
He is small so people do not think about him.		

4 '*But just as Teddy was stooping …*'

Which of the words below is closest in meaning to *stooping*?
Tick **one** box. [1]

Try swapping words and checking that the sentence still makes good sense.

stroking ☐   talking ☐

bending ☐   wriggling ☐

Unit 4

Name _____

Class _____

1 '… *but the karait's wicked little dusty grey head lashed* …'

What does the word *lashed* tell you about the way in which the snake moved? Tick **one** box. [1]

rocking side-to-side ☐   suddenly and violently ☐

with a stick in its mouth ☐

2 Give **two** reasons why Rikki-tikki is important to the family. [2]

> Use all the information on the page. Think about how Teddy behaves with him.

1. _____

2. _____

3 Draw lines to match the character to what they do, in the battle between snake and mongoose.
The first one has been done for you. [2]

Character	Action
Teddy	rushes to attack snake
mother	calls to his parents
father	jumps on enemy's back
mongoose	lunges too far
snake	cries out in a piercing way

(Teddy is matched to 'calls to his parents')

4 '*A full meal makes a slow mongoose.*'

How does this statement explain Rikki-tikki's actions at the end of the fight? [2]

_____

_____

Name _____

Class _____

Unit 4

1 a) How do mongooses win fights with snakes in the old books? [1]

_____

b) How do mongooses win fights with snakes in this story? [1]

_____

2 '… *the mongoose has a jump that is more wonderful than a magical herb.*'

What does this tell you about the jump of a mongoose? Mark each answer as true or false. The first one has been done for you. [2]

	True	False
It is even better than a cure for snake poison.	✓	
It even cures snake bites.		
It is like a magic potion.		
It is better than the explanation in the old books.		

3 How does the author make you realise just how dangerous the fight with the karait was for Rikki-tikki? Give examples from the text. [3]

_____

_____

_____

_____

Think about the fight from Rikki-tikki's viewpoint.

Unit 5

Monarch Butterflies

Monarch butterflies are stunning creatures that live in the USA and Mexico. Their wings have striking patterns in orange, black and white. Some people think the Monarch's bright colours might attract predators, but they actually protect the butterfly. The colours show predators that the butterfly is poisonous to eat and so they leave it alone.

The word *monarch* means king or queen.

Did you know?

A male Monarch butterfly has a black spot on the inside of one of its wings. The female Monarch does not have this spot.

Life cycle of a Monarch butterfly

In March and April, the Monarch lays its eggs on milkweed plants. It takes around four days for the eggs to hatch into caterpillars.

The caterpillars spend their time eating milkweed leaves to help them to grow. A caterpillar is capable of eating an entire leaf in under five minutes! During its caterpillar stage, the Monarch gains around 2,700 times its original weight.

The caterpillar sheds its skin an amazing five times before creating a chrysalis. After about two weeks, the caterpillar spins silk and attaches itself to a branch. It then forms a chrysalis.

Milkweed is a plant with pink flowers.

Fluttery Fact!

The milkweed leaves that the caterpillar eats contain a poisonous chemical. It does not harm the caterpillar but it does make the caterpillar taste horrible to predators. The chemical stays in the adult butterfly's body too.

Inside the chrysalis, the caterpillar starts to change. After ten days, the adult butterfly emerges from the chrysalis. The butterfly flies away to feed on flowers.

A *chrysalis* is a hard shell. It is said like this: *kris-uh-lis.*

Fluttery Fact!
A Monarch butterfly flaps its wings slower than any other butterfly!

The Monarch butterflies that emerge in the spring and summer only live between two and six weeks. Before they die, they lay their eggs on a milkweed plant.

Monarchs that emerge in the autumn have a much longer lifespan. These Monarchs migrate so they can survive the winter in warmer areas. Thousands of Monarchs migrate together in huge swarms. They live for six to eight months, and then come home again to lay their eggs on a milkweed plant the following spring.

Fluttery Fact!
Monarch butterflies have different names. They used to be called *King Billy*, after a king known as *William of Orange*. Some people call them *milkweed butterflies*, and others call them *wanderers*.

Unit 5

Name _____

Class _____

1 How can you tell the difference between a male and female Monarch butterfly? [1]

You'll find the information in a Did you know? box.

_____

2 According to the text, what do the bright wings of the Monarch do? Tick **one** box. [1]

attract predators ☐

tell predators that the butterfly is poisonous ☐

poison predators ☐

help it hide on flowers ☐

3 How is the Monarch different from other butterflies? [1]

_____

_____

4 What other names do people give the Monarch butterfly? Find **three** names. [1]

1. _____

2. _____

3. _____

5 Look at the *Life cycle of a Monarch butterfly* section. **Find** and **copy one** word that means the same as *comes out*. [1]

Try swapping the words and checking the meaning makes sense.

_____

28 © Pearson Education Limited 2018 — Pinpoint English Comprehension Year 4

Name _____

Class _____

Unit 5

1 *'Their wings have striking patterns in orange, black and white.'*

What does the word *striking* tell you about their wings? Tick **one** box. [1]

they are eye-catching ☐   they are poisonous ☐

they are painful ☐   they are triangular ☐

2 Find **two** facts that tell you about the rapid growth of the caterpillar. [2]

> Look for information about the caterpillar's size and weight.

1. _____

2. _____

3 Mark these statements about milkweed plants as true or false. The first one has been done for you. [2]

	True	False
Its leaves contain a poisonous chemical.	✓	
The poisonous chemical kills caterpillars.		
The poisonous chemical kills predators.		
The poison leaves the body of the caterpillar.		

4 Number these facts about the caterpillar 1–4 in the correct order. The first one has been done for you. [1]

attaches itself to a branch with silk ☐   sheds its skin five times ☐ 1

leaves the chrysalis as a butterfly ☐   forms a chrysalis ☐

© Pearson Education Limited 2018   Pinpoint English Comprehension Year 4   29

Unit 5   D

Name _____

Class _____

1 a) Which word best describes the author's view of Monarch butterflies? Circle **one**. [1]

The facts are in different sections so check back through the whole text.

The author thinks Monarch butterflies are …

special   dangerous   Mexican   ordinary

b) Explain your answer, giving evidence from the text. [2]

I think this because _____

_____

_____

2 What does *huge swarm* tell you about the way that Monarch butterflies migrate? [1]

_____

_____

3 Draw lines to match the facts to the time when Monarch butterflies emerge. The first one has been done for you. [2]

Be careful: one fact links with both times.

Time butterflies emerge	Monarch facts
spring and summer	live between six and eight months
	travel in huge swarms
	migrate to warmer places
autumn	lay eggs on milkweed plant
	live between two and six weeks

30   © Pearson Education Limited 2018   *Pinpoint English Comprehension Year 4*

Heartsong

By Kevin Crossley-Holland

When I drew the bow across her bottom string, the viola didn't sing and she didn't miaow or neigh. She brayed like a donkey. Father Antonio winced as if he were sucking a lemon, but then he laughed.

'Everyone's the same,' he exclaimed. 'My music room's a bestiary. I really must compose something for cats and horses and donkeys and mice and pigeons and mosquitoes and winged lions.' The music master waved his arms and roared. 'And all the other creatures in Venice!'

'Compose one for the larks, Father Antonio,' Sister Cattina suggested.

'Larks,' he repeated. 'Violins, then. Just for violins.'

'Or lobsters!' Sister Cattina said, making her fingers into claws.

'Yes!' exclaimed Father Antonio. 'Clicking and clacking. And whistling when you drop them into the pot.'

***

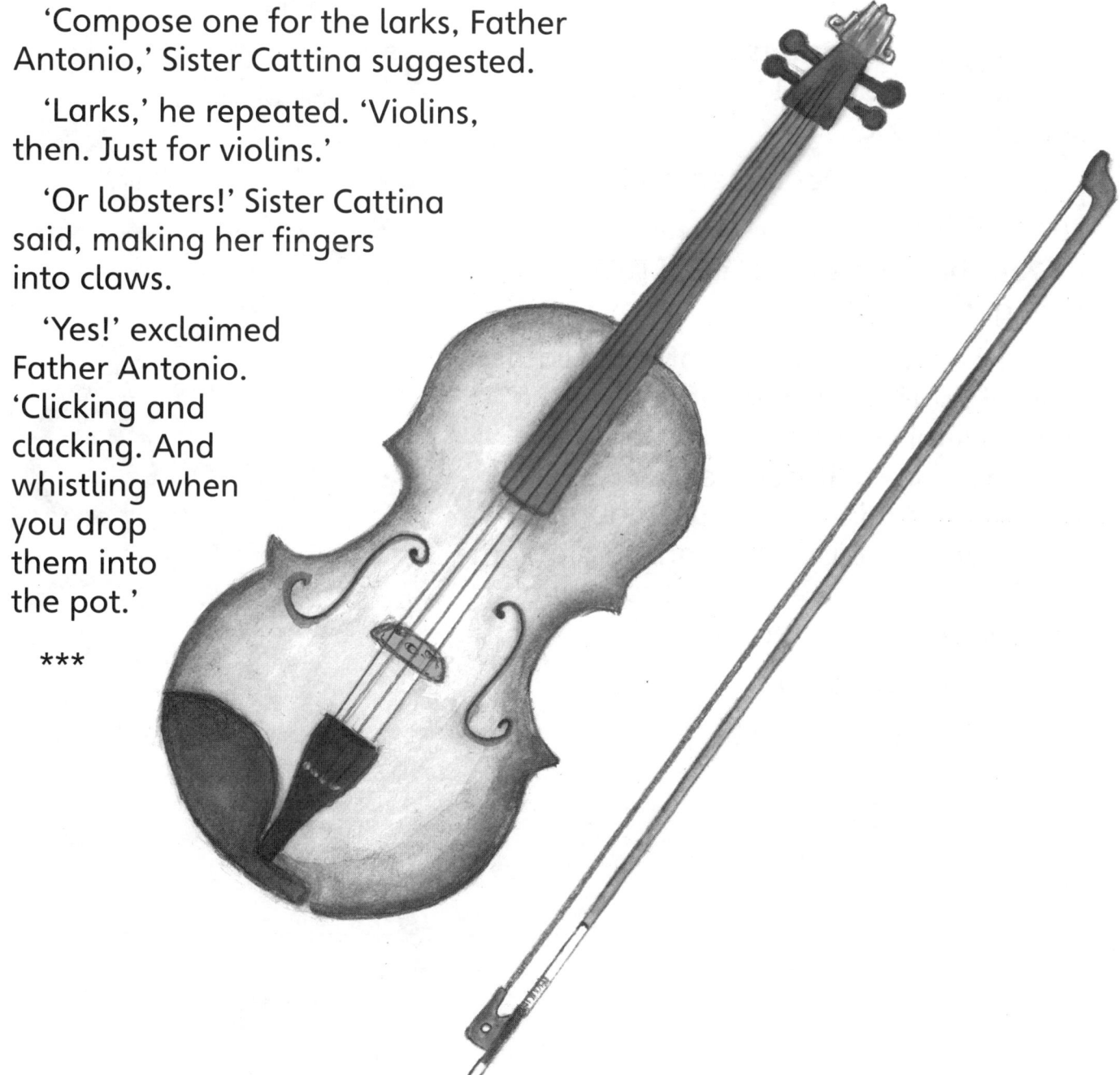

Unit 6

Heartsong

After I had drawn the bow across the C string and the G, and then the D and A strings, Father Antonio pushed out his lower lip. He walked over to the long table and picked up another instrument.

'This is a flute,' Father Antonio told me. 'A beak flute, because her mouthpiece looks like a beak! Her song is more lovely than any other instrument.'

He placed the flute between my hands.

'She makes a beautiful, breathy, birdlike song. I want you to learn to play her.'

Gently I blew, and the flute began to sing. I heard her. I heard her song breathing.

The music master closed his eyes. He smiled.

'Yes,' he said slowly. 'Yes, I rather thought so.'

I'll never forget a word of what Father Antonio said next: 'Some things in our lives, we think about, we hope for, we dream of, we half-believe. But some we just know. And what I know, Laura, is that if you practise and learn to play this instrument, the day will come when angels stop and listen to you.'

That's what he said.

My eyes grew hot with tears.

Name _____

Class _____

Unit 6

❶ With what does the narrator compare the noise she makes with the viola? Tick **one** box. [1]

   a lemon ☐   a donkey ☐

   a bow ☐   a laugh ☐

Read the first paragraph carefully.

❷ What job does Father Antonio do? Tick **one** box. [1]

   zookeeper ☐   cook ☐

   music master ☐   professional dad ☐

❸ What is the narrator's name, and how do you know? [2]

_____

_____

❹ Number these events from the story 1-4 in the correct order.
The first one has been done for you. [1]

Read carefully right to the end.

She plays the viola badly. ☐ 1

The sister joins in the fun. ☐

Father Antonio laughs. ☐

Father Antonio gives her a flute. ☐

Unit 6

Name _____

Class _____

1. *'Father Antonio winced as if he were sucking a lemon, but then he laughed.'*

   What does this tell you about Father Antonio's feelings when he heard the viola? Give **two** answers. [2]

   1. _____

   2. _____

2. *'"Everyone's the same, …"'*

   What does Father Antonio mean when he says this? Explain in detail. [2]

   > Think about what has *just* happened in this scene.

   _____

   _____

3. Look at the second section of the story. **Find** and **copy** a **group of words** that tells you that Father Antonio is thinking to himself about his choice of instrument. [1]

   _____

4. What does Father Antonio think about the flute as a musical instrument? Tick **one** box. [1]

   The flute looks like a bird. ☐

   The flute makes the loveliest music. ☐

   > The answer is in what he says.

   The flute sounds like breathing. ☐

   The flute is the most beautiful-looking instrument. ☐

Name _____

Class _____

Unit 6

1. '"My music room's a bestiary."'
   Which of the following is closest in meaning to *bestiary*, as it is used here. Tick **one** box. [1]

   a collection of animals ☐   only for really good friends ☐

   the greatest room ☐   full of strange noises ☐

2. Why does Sister Cattina make her fingers into claws? [1]
   _____
   _____

3. What is the difference between Father Antonio's reaction to Laura trying the viola, and his reaction to her trying the flute? Use evidence from the text to help you answer. [2]
   _____
   _____
   _____

4. What impression does this text give you of Father Antonio? Choose **one** description, then give evidence to support your choice. [3]

   He is a music-lover. ☐   He is a good teacher. ☐

   He is fun-loving. ☐

   I think this because _____
   _____
   _____

© Pearson Education Limited 2018   Pinpoint English Comprehension Year 4

Unit 7

Stargazing

What are stars?

A star is a bright ball of very hot gas called plasma. There are approximately 200–400 billion stars in the Milky Way. The closest star to Earth is the Sun.

Red dwarfs are the most common star. They burn gas very slowly so they live longer than any other type of star. Red dwarfs are cooler than most stars so they do not shine as brightly.

Type of star	Description
red dwarf star	They are cooler than most stars because they burn fuel slowly.
yellow dwarf star	Medium-sized stars that burn fuel faster than a red dwarf star. The Sun is a yellow dwarf star.
blue giant star	These burn fuel very quickly which makes them very hot and extremely bright.
brown dwarf	A dim, glowing object that has never got big enough to become a star.
double star	A combination of two stars that are so close to each other, they look like a single star.

Star fact!
Stars do not actually twinkle. It just looks like they do because of the way the light from them hits the Earth's atmosphere.

What happens when a star dies?

Most stars take millions of years to die. When a star has burned up all of its fuel, it swells into a red giant. Eventually, it blows itself up in a huge explosion. For a while, this explosion shines brighter than all the other stars in the galaxy. It then quickly fades and all that is left is a small spot surrounded by a cloud of gas. The stardust is scattered through space and eventually forms other stars and planets.

Constellations

The patterns that lots of stars make in the sky are known as constellations. In the past, people drew maps of the stars and joined the dots to make pictures of animals, mythical characters and everyday objects. It can be hard to see how some of the constellations represent the things they are named after, but they do help you to recognise the patterns.

Big Dipper

The *Big Dipper* forms a large bowl with a handle. There is also *The Little Dipper* which is a similar shape, only smaller.

> A *dipper* is a pan for scooping up water.

Orion

Orion is one of the brightest and most well-known constellations. It is also known as *The Hunter* because it is named after a hunter from Greek mythology.

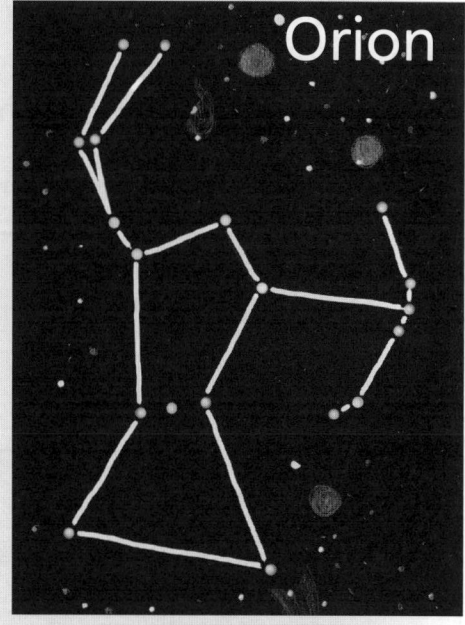

Seven Sisters

The seven stars that form the *Seven Sisters* cluster are easier to spot if you do not look at them. If you *do* look at them directly, they seem to disappear. This is because the nerve cells in the centre of your eye cannot pick up their faint light. If you look to the side of them, you can see them out of the corner of your eye, because the nerve cells at the edge of your eye can see faint light.

Star fact!

The name *Stella* is Latin for star. Can you see a link between the words stella and constellation?

Unit 7

Name _____

Class _____

1 According to the text, what are stars made of? [1]

_____

2 Why are red dwarf stars less bright compared with other stars? Tick **one** box. [1]

They are not shiny. ☐

They are cooler. ☐

They are made of plasma. ☐

They are darker. ☐

> The answer can be found early on in the text.

3 Mark these facts about constellations as true or false. The first one has been done for you. [2]

> Read the paragraph headed *Constellations* carefully.

	True	False
A constellation is a pattern made by some stars.	✓	
Stars can join up in the shape of everyday things.		
Constellations are quite a new idea.		
The Big Dipper is a constellation in the shape of a roller coaster.		

4 Give **two** names for a well-known constellation that gets its name from Greek mythology. [2]

1. _____

2. _____

38 © Pearson Education Limited 2018   Pinpoint English Comprehension Year 4

Name _____

Class _____

Unit 7

1 Place these stars in order of how fast they burn, from the fastest to slowest. [1]

Use the information given in the table.

yellow dwarf   blue giant   red dwarf

_____

_____

2 Look at the table of stars and their descriptions. **Find** and **copy one** word that could be replaced with *blend* or *mixture*. [1]

_____

3 Why might some stargazers argue with the idea of a brown dwarf being a type of star? Give **two** reasons. [2]

1. _____

2. _____

4 The following statements show the events that take place when a star dies. Number them 1-6 to show the correct sequence. The first one has been done for you. [1]

The stardust scatters.	☐	New stars are formed.	☐
It blows itself up.	☐	It expands to a red giant.	☐
It burns up all its fuel.	1	A small spot forms.	☐

© Pearson Education Limited 2018   *Pinpoint English Comprehension Year 4*   39

Unit 7

Name _____

Class _____

1 a) How are the names of constellations helpful? [1]

_____

b) What problem do people sometimes have with them? [1]

_____

2 Do stars twinkle? Answer the question, using evidence from the text. [1]

Look in the Star Fact! boxes.

_____

_____

3 a) What is unusual about the way in which the *Seven Sisters* cluster can be spotted? [1]

_____

_____

b) Explain why this happens, according to the text. [2]

_____

_____

4 Which of the following would make the best replacement title for this text? Tick **one** box. [1]

Orion's Belt ☐   Star Colours ☐

Stars and Constellations ☐   Get the Most from Your Telescope ☐

Alice's Adventures in Wonderland

Unit 8

An excerpt adapted from the original by Lewis Carroll.

Alice spots a white rabbit with a pocket watch running past her in a hurry. The rabbit can talk! Alice follows the rabbit down a rabbit hole.

The rabbit hole went straight on like a tunnel for some way and then dipped down suddenly. Alice found herself falling down a very deep well.

Either the well was very deep or she fell very slowly for she had plenty of time as she went down. First, she tried to look down because she wanted to see what was coming next, but it was too dark. Then she looked at the sides of the well and saw that they were filled with cupboards and bookshelves. She took down a jar from one of the shelves which said 'ORANGE MARMALADE', but it was empty. She did not want to drop the jar and managed to put it into a cupboard as she fell past.

Down, down, down. Would the fall never come to an end? 'I wonder how many miles I've fallen now?' she said aloud. 'I must be getting close to the centre of the Earth, and that would be four thousand miles down, I think.'

Down, down, down. There was nothing else to do so Alice soon began talking again, 'Dinah will miss me very much tonight, I think!' (Dinah was Alice's pet cat.) 'I hope they'll remember her. They should give her a saucer of milk at tea-time. Dinah my dear! I wish you were down here with me. There are no mice in the air but you might catch a bat. That's like a mouse, you know, but do cats eat bats, I wonder?' Here Alice began to get rather sleepy. She went on talking to herself in a dreamy sort of way, 'Do cats eat bats? Do bats eat cats?' She felt that she was dozing off. Then suddenly, thump! thump! Down she came, landing on a heap of sticks and dry leaves. The fall was over.

Unit 8: Alice's Adventures in Wonderland

Alice was not hurt at all and was up on her feet in a moment. She looked up, but it was all dark overhead. Ahead of her was another long passage and the White Rabbit was hurrying down it. There was not a moment to lose! Away went Alice like the wind! She was just in time to hear it say, as it turned a corner, 'Oh my ears and whiskers, how late it's getting!' She was close behind it when she turned the corner, but the rabbit was not there. She found herself in a long, low hall lit up by a row of lamps hanging from the roof.

There were doors all round the hall but they were all locked. When Alice had been all the way down one side and up the other, trying every door, she walked sadly down the middle. She wondered how she would ever get out again.

Suddenly, she came upon a little three-legged table made of solid glass. There was nothing sat on it except a tiny golden key. Alice's first thought was that it might belong to one of the doors, but either the locks were too large or the key was too small. She then came upon a low curtain she had not noticed before. Behind the curtain was a little door about fifteen inches high. She tried the little golden key in the lock and to her great delight it fitted!

Name _____

Class _____

Unit 8

1 '*Away went Alice like the wind!*'
Why has the author used *like the wind!* to to describe how Alice moved? [1]

Find the sentence in the text and read around it for clues.

_____
_____

2 What is Alice worrying about as she falls down the tunnel? [1]

_____

Think about what Alice was trying to do before she felt sad.

3 '*... she walked sadly down the middle.*'
Why was Alice feeling sad at this point in the story? Mark each statement as true or false.
The first one has been done for you. [2]

	True	False
All the doors were locked.	✓	
There seemed to be no way out.		
She was missing the rabbit.		
She was missing her parents.		

4 Number these events from the story 1-6 in the correct order.
The first one has been done for you. [1]

Alice finds a key.	☐	Alice starts to fall asleep.	☐
Alice falls down a hole.	1	Alice sees the rabbit again.	☐
Alice lands on sticks and leaves.	☐	Alice takes an empty jar of marmalade.	☐

© Pearson Education Limited 2018   *Pinpoint English Comprehension Year 4*   43

Unit 8

Name _____

Class _____

1 Why does Alice start talking to herself? Give **two** reasons. [2]

Re-read the fourth paragraph carefully.

1. _____

2. _____

2 '... *the White Rabbit was hurrying*'

How else do you know that the rabbit is in a rush? Give **two** ways. [2]

1. _____

2. _____

3 When the rabbit disappears around the corner, Alice finds herself in a hall. Mark each statement about the hall as true or false. The first one has been done for you. [2]

Read the last two paragraphs very carefully.

	True	False
It is in complete darkness.		✓
It is like a long corridor.		
It has many locked doors.		
It has a high ceiling.		
It has a low curtain behind which is a door.		

4 **Find** and **copy** the **group of words** to show Alice's feeling of relief when the key fits. [1]

_____

Name _____

Class _____

Unit **8**

1 How can you tell that Alice is falling for a long time? Give **three** ways. [3]

1. _____

2. _____

3. _____

2 What type of story is *Alice in Wonderland*? Tick **one** box. [1]

a fantasy ☐   a horror ☐

a traditional tale ☐   a myth ☐

Think about all the elements of the story.

3 Apart from the talking rabbit, give **three** other things that are very unusual about the story. [3]

1. _____

2. _____

3. _____

4 From her actions, thoughts and words in the text, which words would best describe Alice's personality? Circle **two** words and explain your answers with evidence from the text. [3]

selfish   thoughtful   brave   curious   cowardly

_____

_____

_____

© Pearson Education Limited 2018   Pinpoint English Comprehension Year 4

Unit 9

Taking the Shot

I have always hated matches that come down to the last few seconds. I cannot stand watching them, and I cannot stand playing in them. I feel really anxious knowing that anything can still happen and the game might end in disappointment.

So you can imagine how it felt to have about one minute left on the clock in our football match last weekend. We were playing against the Rovers, and we were down by one goal. We desperately wanted to score before the final whistle. If only we could equalise, the game would go into extra time and we would still have a chance of winning.

> To *equalise* means to get a goal that gives you the same score as the other side.

This was an important match. The winner would go through to the county championships. It was a very tense time.

I was playing the forward position that day. I was kicking the ball up the field with my friend, Alex. We were passing it to and fro, making good progress. I could hear the crowd cheering and I even heard people yelling my name. I was very focused. I kept my eye on the goal. I was looking for any opening to take a shot. I knew the goalie was a bit slow, so if I could shoot quickly, the ball might just slip past him. It was my only hope.

In an instant, I saw my chance. I couldn't believe my luck! There was a clear line straight through to the net and the ball was right at my feet, ready to take a glorious flight to the back of the net. I was in the perfect position, and the opposition's defenders were nowhere to be seen. All I needed to do was to keep my cool and put in a hard, well-aimed kick. I was sure that the ball would sail straight past the goalie.

> The *opposition* is the team you are playing against.

I took a deep breath, planted my left foot and aimed my right leg toward the goal. I whacked that ball with all my strength. I watched the ball as if it were in slow motion. It shot through the air, straight and fast, directly towards the goal … and right into the goalie's hands. As he rolled on the ground, cradling the ball, the full-time whistle blew its mocking sound.

The match was over. We had lost. I have never felt such disappointment in my life. It didn't matter that my coach gave me a high-five and told me I'd played well, or that my team mates kept saying, "Nice try!". I had wanted to win so badly. But when everything came down to me, I had missed the crucial shot.

Unit 9

Name _____

Class _____

1 Number these events from the story 1-5 in the correct order. The first one has been done for you. [1]

He kicks the ball as hard as he can. ☐

The coach high-fives him. ☐

The goalie catches the ball. ☐

He sees a clear line to the net. ☐ 1

The whistle blows. ☐

Read the whole extract and notice when each of these things happens.

2 Look at the third paragraph. Why was it particularly important to win this match? [1]

_____

3 **Find** and **copy** the **group of words** that tell you that he spots the clear line all of a sudden. [1]

_____

4 'All I needed to do was keep my cool …'

What is meant by *keep my cool* as it is used here? Mark each answer as true or false. The first one has been done for you. [2]

Read the scene and think about how he is feeling as he thinks this.

	True	False
drink some cold water		✓
not panic		
lower my temperature		
keep calm		

48 © Pearson Education Limited 2018   Pinpoint English Comprehension Year 4

Name _____

Class _____

Unit 9

1. How do you know that the narrator and Alex are playing well together? Tick **one** box. [1]

   They were passing and making good progress. ☐

   They were winning by one goal with a minute left. ☐

   The coach was high-fiving them. ☐

   They were in the forward position today. ☐

2. '*It was my only hope.*'
   What was his *only hope*? [1]

   Read what he says before that line.

   _____

3. With which foot does the narrator take the shot? [1]

   _____

4. '*… my coach gave me a high-five … my team mates kept saying, "Nice try"*'
   What does this information tell you about the narrator's team? [1]

   Re-read the end and think about how everyone is feeling.

   _____
   _____

5. Look at the last paragraph. **Find** and **copy one** word that means *most important*. [1]

   _____

© Pearson Education Limited 2018   *Pinpoint English Comprehension Year 4*   **49**

Unit 9

Name _____

Class _____

1 **Find** and **copy** the **group of words** that makes it seem as though the whistle was laughing at his failure. [1]

_____

2 What is different about the first paragraph compared with the rest of the story? Finish both of these sentences.

> Think about what he is telling you in the first paragraph. Don't write more than a sentence for each.

a) The first paragraph is about … [1]

_____

b) In the rest of the story, he is telling you about … [1]

_____

3 How does the author feel in the second paragraph? How do you know?
How does he feel in the last paragraph? How do you know? [3]

_____

_____

_____

_____

4 Which of the following would work **best** as a replacement title for *Taking the Shot*? [1]

| The Match Last Week | ☐ | My Biggest Disappointment | ☐ |
| I Am So Tense | ☐ | The Perfect Goal | ☐ |

Unit 10

I Like to Stay Up

By Grace Nichols

I like to stay up
and listen
when big people talking
jumbie stories

I does feel
so tingly and excited
inside me

Jumbie is a Guyanese word for *ghost*.

But when my mother say
"Girl, time for bed"

Then is when
I does feel a dread

Then is when
I does jump into me bed

Then is when
I does cover up
from me feet to me head

Then is when
I does wish I didn't listen
to no stupid jumbie story

Then is when I does wish I read
me book instead

From *Under the Moon and Over the Sea*

Unit 10

Name _____

Class _____

1 Number these events from the poem 1–5 to put them in the right order. The first one has been done for you. [1]

She covers herself up. ☐   She listens to some ghost stories. [1]

She jumps into bed. ☐   She feels scared. ☐

She gets sent to bed. ☐

2 *'so tingly and excited'*

What does *tingly* mean here? Tick **one** box. [1]

sick ☐   thrilled ☐

terrified ☐   anxious ☐

Try swapping words and checking that the sentence still makes the same sense.

3 Which line of the poem tells you that she makes sure that the bedclothes cover her up completely? [1]

_____

4 *'Then is when I does wish I read Me book instead'*

Instead of doing what? Explain what she is wishing, and why. [2]

Read the last verse and don't forget to explain it.

_____

_____

Name _____

Class _____

Unit 10

1 Look at the first verse. How does she experience the ghost stories? Tick **one** box. [1]

Read the first verse carefully.

Adults are telling them. ☐

Adults are reading them. ☐

They are on TV. ☐

They are on at the cinema. ☐

2 '*I does feel a dread*' What word could you use here that is similar in meaning to *dread*? [1]

_____

3 Why might she call the jumbie stories stupid? Mark these exlanations as true or false. The first one has been done for you. [2]

	True	False
She is cross with the ghost stories.		✓
She thinks ghost stories are rubbish.		
She thinks ghost stories are for silly people.		
She is cross with herself for listening to them.		

4 Draw lines to match the short descriptions of some verses to the verse number. The first two have been done for you. [2]

Verse number	Description
3	dread
2	wishes she didn't listen
7	sent to bed
4	listening
1	excited

© Pearson Education Limited 2018   *Pinpoint English Comprehension Year 4*   53

Unit 10 D

Name _____

Class _____

1 a) Look at the last two verses. At what point does she change from enjoying the exciting jumbie stories, to being scared? [1]

_____

b) Why does this happen? [2]

_____
_____
_____

Read through carefully and think about when the change happens, and what causes it too.

2 Why do you think the poem is written in the first person (using *I*) rather than third person (using *she*)? [2]

_____
_____

3 Which of the below would work as a replacement title for *I Like to Stay Up*? [1]

Jumbie Fun ☐

From Fun to Fear ☐

Reading about Ghosts ☐

Jumping into Bed ☐

54 © Pearson Education Limited 2018   Pinpoint English Comprehension Year 4

My Dad's a Birdman

By David Almond

An ordinary spring morning in 12 Lark Lane. The birds were tweeting and whistling outside. The city traffic rumbled and roared. Lizzie's alarm went ringadingding. She jumped out of bed, washed her face, scrubbed behind her ears, brushed her teeth, brushed her hair, put on her uniform, went downstairs, filled the kettle, switched it on, put bread in the toaster, set the table with two plates, two mugs, two knives, milk and butter and jam, then she went to the foot of the stairs.

"Dad!" she shouted. "Daddy!"

No answer.

"Dad! Time to get up!"

No answer.

"If you don't get up now, I'll come up there and …"

She stepped heavily onto the first step, then onto the second step.

"I'm on me way!" she shouted.

Unit 11

My Dad's a Birdman

She heard a grunt and a groan, then nothing.

"I'll count to five. One … two … two and a half … Daddy!"

There was a muffled shout from upstairs.

"Oriyt, Lizzie! Oriyt!"

There was a crash and another groan, then there he was, in a scruffy dressing-gown and his hair all wild and his face all hairy.

"Downstairs now," said Lizzie.

He stumbled down.

"And don't look at me like that."

"No, Lizzie."

She tugged the dressing-gown straight on his shoulders.

"Look at the state of you," she said. "What on earth have you been doing up there?"

He grinned.

"Been dreaming," he said.

"Dreaming! What a man. Now sit at the table. Sit up straight."

"Yes, Lizzie."

He sat down on the edge of a chair. His eyes were shining and excited. Lizzie poured him a mug of tea. "Drink this," she said, and he took a little sip. "And eat that toast." He nibbled at a corner of the toast. "Eat it properly, Dad." He took a bigger bite. "And chew it," she said. He chewed for a moment. "And *swallow* it, Dad."

He grinned. "Yes, Lizzie." He took a big bite, chewed, swallowed and he opened his mouth wide for her to look inside.

"All gone," he said. "See?"

She clicked her tongue and turned her eyes away. "Don't be silly, Dad," she said. Then she smoothed his hair down and brushed it. She straightened the collar of his pyjama jacket. She felt the thick stubble on his chin.

"You've got to look after yourself," she said. "You can't go on the way you are. Can you?"

He shook his head.

"No, Lizzie," he answered. "Certainly not, Lizzie."

"I want you to have a shower and a shave today and to get properly dressed."

"Yes, Lizzie."

"Good. And what plans have you got for today?"

He sat up straight and looked her in the eye.

"I'm going to fly, Lizzie. Just like a bird."

Lizzie rolled her eyes.

"Are you now?" she said.

"Yes, I am. And I'm going to enter the competition."

"Competition? What competition?"

He laughed and leaned forward and held her arm.

"The Great Human Bird Competition, of course! Have you not heard about it? It's coming to town! I heard about it yesterday. No, the day before yesterday. Or that day a week gone last Tuesday. Anyway, the first one to fly across the River Tyne wins a thousand pounds. And I'm going to enter. It's true, Lizzie. It's really true. I'm going to win! I'm going to make me mark at last."

Unit 11

Name _____

Class _____

1 Number these events from the story 1-4 in the correct order. The first one has been done for you. [1]

Lizzie makes sure her father eats some toast. ☐

Lizzie prepares breakfast. ☐

Lizzie wakes her father up. ☐

Lizzie's father says he's going to fly. ☐ 4

2 Mark these statements about Lizzie as true or false. The first one has been done for you. [2]

Read the whole text and think about what she actually says and does.

	True	False
Lizzie asks her dad what he's been dreaming about.		✓
Lizzie is caring for her dad.		
Lizzie gives her dad orders.		
Lizzie asks if her dad is going to enter the competition.		

3 Why does Lizzie start counting? [2]

_____

_____

Read everything she says to her dad before he gets up.

4 'He nibbled at a corner of the toast.'

What does *nibbled* tell you about the way he ate? [1]

_____

Name _____

Class _____

Unit 11

1. **Find** and **copy one** word that shows that Dad was *unsteady* coming down the stairs. [1]

_____

2. '*Then she smoothed his hair down and brushed it. She straightened the collar of his pyjama jacket.*'

   What **two** things does this sentence suggest about Lizzie's relationship with her dad? [2]

   Think about who you would expect to be doing these things.

   1. _____

   2. _____

3. What does Lizzie mean when she says "*You can't go on the way you are*"? Mark each answer as true or false.
   The first one has been done for you. [2]

	True	False
She's going to stop looking after him.		✓
She wants him to change.		
His behaviour has been like this for a while.		
She's furious with him.		

4. '*Lizzie rolled her eyes*'

   What do these words suggest that Lizzie is thinking about her dad's statement? Tick **one** box. [1]

   That's wonderful! ☐   I can just imagine you doing that. ☐

   Oh, no. Here we go again! ☐   It is not like you to say such a thing. ☐

Unit 11 D

Name _____

Class _____

1 *'It was an ordinary spring morning …'*
Why might the author have used the word *ordinary* in this opening sentence? Give **two** reasons. [2]

> Think about what comes after this sentence, and what an *ordinary* morning might be.

1. _____

2. _____

2 What **two** things do you learn about Lizzie's character from the description of her getting up and getting ready? Give evidence from the text. [2]

> Look at the first paragraph carefully.

1. _____
_____

2. _____
_____

3 Lizzie: *'scrubbed behind her ears … put on her uniform …'*

Dad: *'his hair all wild and his face all hairy'*
What might the author be suggesting about each of the characters, from these **two** pieces of evidence? [2]

Lizzie: _____
_____

Dad: _____
_____

The Merry Adventures of Robin Hood

Unit 12

An excerpt adapted from the original by Howard Pyle

Robin Hood was an outlaw. That is why he made Sherwood Forest his home for many years. Two hundred pounds was the reward for any man who would bring Robin Hood into town.

Robin Hood stayed hidden in the woods for a year. In that time, about one hundred good, strong men joined him. They too had been outlawed and mistreated and they chose Robin to be their leader. Now they swore that they would mistreat those who had wronged them. They would steal the money back from rich men that had been taken from the poor.

> An *outlaw* is someone who has to live outside their town because they have broken the law.

After a while, the people saw that Robin and his men meant them no harm. Instead, poor families received money or food from them in times of need. The people praised Robin and his Merry Men and told tales of him and their life in Sherwood Forest. They felt he was one of them.

The Sheriff of Nottingham swore that he himself would capture Robin. The Sheriff did not know about the men Robin had with him, and thought Robin was alone in the forest. He offered 80 golden coins to anyone who would capture Robin.

> A *sheriff* was a type of judge in the past.

Unit 12: The Merry Adventures of Robin Hood

But the men of Nottingham Town knew more than the Sheriff did and laughed to think of capturing the bold outlaw. They knew that they would get cracked heads if they tried. Two weeks went by and no one came forward to do what the Sheriff wanted.

"If only I could get Robin to come to Nottingham Town," thought the Sheriff, "I could grab him myself. He would never get away." Then an idea came to him like a flash. He would hold an archery competition with a big prize that would tempt Robin Hood to come and take part. He slapped his hand on his leg to congratulate himself for plotting such a wonderful plan!

The Sheriff sent his men to tell everyone far and wide about the archery contest. They told people in every town all about it. Anyone who could draw a longbow could try for the prize – an arrow of pure gold.

> *Archery* is the skill of using a bow and arrow. Archery was a useful skill for shooting enemies in battle, and for hunting animals to eat. In a competition, people aim the arrow at a target.

> *To draw* a longbow means preparing to shoot an arrow from a bow by pulling back the string ready to fire it.

Name _____

Class _____

Unit 12

1 How long did Robin Hood stay hidden in the woods? [1]

Read the first paragraph again.

_____

2 Look at the fourth paragraph. How did the Sheriff of Nottingham congratulate himself? Tick **one** box. [1]

| with an archery competition | ☐ | with a slap on the leg | ☐ |
| with a golden arrow | ☐ | with 80 gold coins | ☐ |

3 '… *the bold outlaw*'

Which of the below best matches the meaning of *bold* as it is used here? Tick **one** box. [1]

Check to see which word works best in the sentence.

| angry | ☐ | evil | ☐ |
| brave | ☐ | poor | ☐ |

4 Draw lines to match the characters to the facts about them. The first one has been done for you. [2]

Characters	Facts
Robin Hood	wants to capture Robin
the Merry Men	leads the outlaws
the Sheriff	receive food from Robin
poor families	laugh about catching Robin
men of the town	choose Robin to lead them

© Pearson Education Limited 2018   *Pinpoint English Comprehension Year 4*

Unit 12

Name _____

Class _____

1 *'They too had been outlawed and mistreated.'*
What does the word *too* tell you about the men joining Robin Hood at this point in the story? Tick **one** box. [1]

They had been mistreated very badly. ☐

They had been treated in the same way as Robin. ☐

They were very bad outlaws. ☐

They were very strong, good outlaws. ☐

2 According to the text, when did Robin Hood and his men give money and food to the poor families? [1]

Read the second paragraph carefully.

_____

3 Why did Robin Hood and his men think it was all right to steal from the rich? [1]

_____

_____

4 Mark each explanation of he Sheriff's second plan as true or false. The first one has been done for you. [2]

	True	False
to trap Robin in the town	✓	
to give 80 gold coins to anyone who caught him		
to tempt Robin with a golden arrow		
to shoot Robin with a golden arrow		

Name _____

Class _____

Unit 12

1 According to the first paragraph, how were the Merry Men similar *to* Robin Hood? Tick **two** boxes. [1]

| He was their leader. ☐ | They were good and strong. ☐ |
| They had been outlawed. ☐ | They lived in the woods. ☐ |

2 Why might the Sheriff think that his second plan would get Robin Hood to come into the town? [3]

> Think about what the Sheriff must know about Robin.

_____

_____

_____

3 **Find** and **copy one sentence** in the second paragraph that tells you the people trusted Robin Hood like he was a friend. [1]

_____

4 How did the people of Nottingham show they respected Robin Hood? Mark each answer as true or false by ticking the correct box. [2]

	True	False
They praised him and his men.		
They told tales of his life.		
They chose him as their leader.		
They wanted him to win the golden arrow.		

Unit 13

Natural Measures

In the past, people did not use rulers, scales and clocks to measure things like we do today. Instead, they used parts of the body, seeds and stones to measure the length, volume and weight of different things.

Name	Body part	Used to measure	Modern equivalent
a cubit	the distance from a man's elbow to the middle fingertip	land, buildings	45·7 cm
a foot	the length of a man's foot	wood, furniture	30 cm
a span	the distance from the thumb to the little finger on a spread hand	cloth, furniture	20 cm
a hand	the width of a hand where the four fingers meet the palm	height of a horse	10 cm

Measuring length

In ancient Egypt, length was measured with the cubit. It was used to measure buildings, areas of land and even the level of flooding of the River Nile.

Measuring volume

It is important to know the volume of a container so you know how much it can hold. Imagine you wanted to buy a container of rice, you would want to know how big it was before you paid for it. In the past, people used seeds to measure the volume of a container. They filled the container with seeds, and then counted them.

Measuring weight

People used seeds and stones to measure how heavy things were because many goods were priced according to their weight. Carob seeds were used for weighing diamonds. The weight of a carob seed was called a carat. Gemstones are still measured in carats today. A carat is two tenths (0·2) of a gram.

Unit 13

Measuring time

People use the position of the sun to tell the time. We know that when the sun is high in the sky, it is midday. A sundial can help us to tell the time. Sunlight hits the pointer on a sundial and makes a shadow, and the shadow points to a number which shows the time.

> **Fascinating Fact!**
> The most expensive gemstone ever sold is a 59·6-carat pink diamond known as the *Pink Star*. In 2017, it sold for £53·7 million!

Making measurements match

Although it was easy to use natural objects to measure things, bodies, seeds and stones were not all the same size and weight. This meant measurements were not always accurate.

The Egyptians made a standard cubit stick, which measured 52·4 centimetres. Everybody could measure cubits of the same length using these sticks.

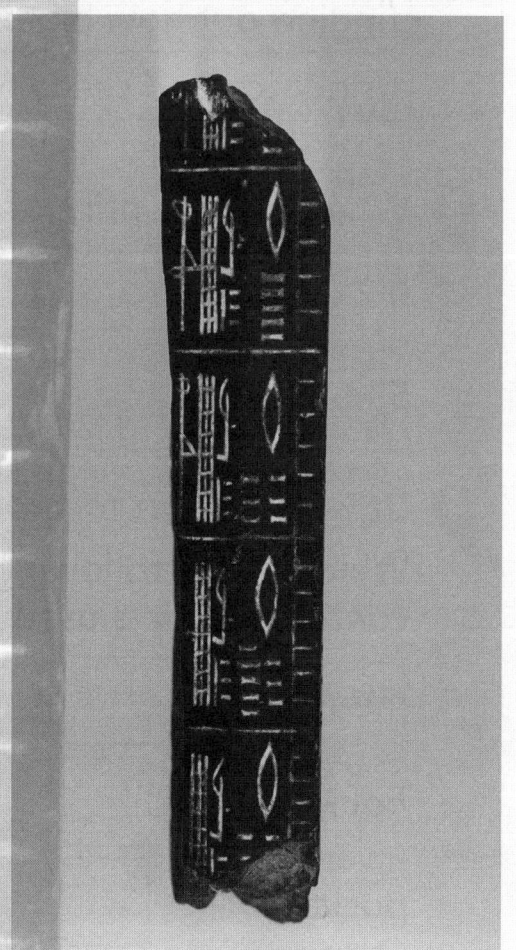

People from different places started to trade goods with each other. They agreed to measure things using the same measurements.

In 1875, many countries agreed to make all measurements the same. So now, a metre in France is exactly the same length as a metre in the UK, for example. People do not use the same units of measurement in all countries. In the UK, distance is usually measured in miles, but in France they use kilometres.

Unit 13

Name _____

Class _____

1 What examples of *natural measures* are given in the first paragraph? [2]

The answer is in the text.

_____

_____

2 What is the section headed *Measuring volume* about? Mark each answer as true or false. The first one has been done for you [2]

	True	False
using seeds as a natural measure	✓	
how loud rice and seeds can be		
finding out how big a container is		
using rice and seeds to measure music		

3 What was the price of the *Pink Star*? Tick **one** box. [1]

0·2 grams ☐   £53·7 million ☐

59·6 carats ☐   2017 ☐

4 '*It is important to know the volume of a container.*'

Which of the following is closest in meaning to *container* as it is used here? Tick **one** box. [1]

meal ☐

holder ☐

pocket ☐

speaker ☐

Swap each word with the word in the sentence and check it still makes good sense.

Name _____

Class _____

Unit 13

1 Why is the text called *Natural Measures*? [1]

Think about what you learn from this text.

_____

_____

2 What have all the measures in the table got in common with each other? [1]

_____

3 Look at the section headed *Measuring weight*. Why was it important that many goods were weighed? Tick **one** box. [1]

| The weight gave the price. ☐ | Carob seeds weigh the same as diamonds. ☐ |

| Diamonds are expensive. ☐ | The weight was the same as the price. ☐ |

4 What are the **three** main things you can learn from the table? [3]

Don't answer with specifics about any of the measures; think about all of the information together.

1. _____

2. _____

3. _____

5 Look at the section headed *Making measurements match*. Why did the Egyptians make a standard cubit stick? [1]

_____

_____

© Pearson Education Limited 2018 *Pinpoint English Comprehension Year 4* **69**

Unit 13 D

Name _____

Class _____

1 Look at the table column headed *Modern equivalent*. Which of the following is closest in meaning to *modern equivalent* as it is used in the table? Tick **one** box. [1]

measures up to ☐

new distance ☐

the same amount today ☐

units of measure ☐

2 Why do you think a sundial is a better way to tell the time than looking at the position of the sun in the sky? [2]

Read the Measuring time section and explain in detail.

_____

_____

3 Look at the section headed *Making measurements match*.

a) What was really helpful about natural measures? [1]

_____

b) What was the big problem with natural measures? [1]

_____

4 According to the text, why did people start to agree on using the same measures? [1]

_____

_____

My Lemonade Stand

Day 1

It was a hot day in the summer holidays and I had nothing to do. It should have been perfect but I was bored! There was nothing that I *had* to do, but there was nothing that I *wanted* to do, either.

My dad wandered by. "Whatever's wrong?" he asked. "You look like you've been sucking lemons!" He picked up an unevenly shaped yellow fruit from a dish on the kitchen worktop and tossed it across the room to me. "There you go! Enjoy another one!" he chuckled.

I caught the missile, unamused by Dad's feeble attempt to cheer me up. Then I had an idea. No one wants to suck lemons but even in my grumpy mood the thought of a tall glass of delicious home-made lemonade was appealing. Gran's recipe was right there on the fridge door, so I rounded up the ingredients and made a start.

It was great fun making the lemonade, but then – what a bore! I had to leave it overnight before it would be ready to drink!

Day 2

I asked my friends to come over and try my lemonade. It was fantastic, but we soon hit a problem. I hadn't made enough and we ran out. I went shopping for a lot more lemons, and made a very big batch ready for the next day.

My dad told me that when he was a boy, he used to sell homemade lemonade to earn some pocket money.

Lemonade (makes 5 glasses)

3 unwaxed lemons
140 g caster sugar
1 litre water

1. Squeeze the lemons and put the juice in a large jug.
2. Add the sugar.
3. Ask an adult to carefully add 500 ml of hot water. Stir until all the sugar has dissolved.
4. Add 500 ml of cold water and stir.
5. Cover and chill overnight. Serve with ice and slices of lemon.

Unit 14

My Lemonade Stand

Day 3

My friends came back for more lemonade, and they brought their friends too. This time, I was better prepared. I had set up a stall with jugs of lemonade, ice, paper cups and a sign: HOMEMADE LEMONADE – 50p A CUP.

I nearly sold out! But would it work again the next day? What if everyone was fed up with lemonade? Then my dad had another suggestion, "Why don't you try adding blueberries? I bet they would all love blue lemonade!"

What a fantastic idea! I counted up my earnings and invested some of the money in more lemons, sugar, paper cups and blueberries. Then I got to work again.

Day 4

It turns out that blueberry lemonade isn't blue, it's a deep pinky-red. It's also delicious and a very big hit! Soon I was back to the shops spending more of my profits on more ingredients, but I was confident that I would earn it back when I sold my next batch.

Day 5

I have jugs and jugs of blueberry lemonade, a beautiful stall, stacks of paper cups … and no customers! It's a miserable rainy day and no one wants lemonade today. What a disaster! I've spent most of my profits, and I'm stuck with all this lemonade I can't sell.

"How about ice lollies?" Dad suggested. "You can sell them when it's sunny again."

So, it's back to the shops for me to invest what's left of my profits in ice lolly trays!

Name _____

Class _____

Unit 14

1 Look at *Day 1*. Why is the writer bored? [1]

_____

_____

There are two reasons – look in the first paragraph.

2 Look at *Day 2*. Mark these explanations of the problem as true or false. The first one has been done for you. [2]

	True	False
They had to leave the lemonade overnight.		✓
There were not enough friends.		
There was not enough lemonade.		
They had to go shopping.		
They soon ran out of all the writer's drink.		

3 When did Dad sell lemonade? [1]

_____

_____

4 Look at *Day 4*. **Find** and **copy** the **group of words** that tells you the blueberry lemonade was *extremely popular*. [1]

Try swapping the words and check the sentence still makes good sense.

_____

© Pearson Education Limited 2018   *Pinpoint English Comprehension Year 4*   73

Unit 14

Name _____

Class _____

1 'I caught the missile.'
What was the *missile*? [1]

_____

_____

The clues to the first and second question are in *Day 1*. Re-read the whole section carefully.

2 Look at *Day 1*. Give **two** pieces of evidence that show you Dad was in a good mood. [2]

1. _____

2. _____

3 Look at *Day 1*. **Find** and **copy one** word that tells you the writer thought the idea of fresh lemonade was *delightful*. [1]

_____

4 'But then – what a bore!'
What was *a bore*? Mark each answer as true or false. The first one has been done for you. [2]

	True	False
leaving the lemonade overnight	✓	
cleaning up afterwards		
making the lemonade		
it was not ready to drink immediately		

Name _____

Class _____

Unit 14

1 '... *Dad's feeble attempt to cheer me up.*'
What is Dad's *feeble attempt*? [1]

Think about the whole scene.

_____
_____

2 In addition to *feeble* what word tells you that the writer does not think Dad's joke is funny? [1]

_____

3 What evidence is there that Dad is a good problem solver? Give **three** examples from the text. [3]

1. _____

2. _____

3. _____

4 Look at *Day 5*.

a) Why can't the writer sell blueberry lemonade on Day 5? [1]

Answer both parts of the question and think about why the writer is feeling this way.

_____
_____

b) Why is this a disaster? [1]

_____
_____

Unit 15

Sleeping for Survival

Hibernation

Many animals take a long rest during the winter months. This is called hibernating. Animals have a very deep sleep that can last for months. It helps them to survive the coldest time of year as it takes a lot of energy to stay warm in the winter. If animals cannot find food, they will not have enough energy to keep warm and they may not survive. For some animals, the answer to this problem is to hibernate during the winter when food is scarce.

While an animal is hibernating its body temperature drops, its heart rate and breathing slow down, and it does not eat or go to the toilet. It stays in a very deep sleep and cannot wake up easily. It does not wake up until the temperature rises enough in spring. The rise in temperature signals that food is available again.

How long do animals hibernate for?

The length of hibernation varies from animal to animal. In the UK, bats hibernate for about four months. They shelter in caves, trees, tunnels, bridges or roof spaces.

Hedgehogs build themselves a nest of dry leaves and twigs under hedges, in old rabbit holes or under sheds. They may hibernate for up to five or six months in a very cold winter. If a hedgehog is not carrying enough fat on its body when it hibernates, or wakes up too soon, it may not have enough energy stored in its body to survive the winter.

Unit 15

> **Survival Fact!**
> If you accidentally disturb a hibernating hedgehog, you should cover it up with leaves and put some water and cat or dog food nearby.

Ladybirds hibernate for five or six months. They often huddle together in groups on tree bark, under leaves, in sheds, garages and even inside houses. A house is not a good place for ladybirds to hibernate. If the warmth wakes them up during the winter there is nothing for them to eat and they starve to death. It is best to move ladybirds that are trying to hibernate into a sheltered place outside.

To huddle together means to cuddle up close.

Summer hibernation

Many people think that animals only hibernate in the winter but some animals take a long sleep in the summer instead. They are trying to survive the hot, dry weather when there is little or no water. A summer sleep is called aestivation.

Frogs are cold-blooded animals. This means that they cannot make themselves warmer or cooler than their surroundings. In very hot places some species of frogs would not be able to keep cool enough to survive the summers, so they bury themselves under a log or a rock where they aestivate to survive the summer heat.

Both hibernation and aestivation help animals survive in the harshest climates on Earth.

Unit 15

Name _____

Class _____

1 According to the text, what is hibernation? [1]

_____

2 Give **two** reasons why some animals hibernate. [2]

Think about how the time of year can affect some animals.

1. _____

2. _____

3 Draw lines to match the animals to their hibernation or aestivation behaviours. The first one has been done for you. [2]

You'll need to look for these animals throughout the whole text.

Animal	Hibernation facts
bats	up to 6 months in a cold winter
hedgehogs	aestivate if really hot, under logs
ladybirds	4-6 months, in caves
frogs	5-6 months, huddled together

4 **Find** and **copy one** word very near the end of the text that means *toughest*. [1]

_____

5 Circle the names of the animals in this list which hibernate. [1]

bats   hedgehogs   ladybirds

bears   moles   cats

78 © Pearson Education Limited 2018   *Pinpoint English Comprehension Year 4*

Name _____

Class _____

Unit 15

1 What happens to the body of an animal during hibernation? Give **three** examples. [3]

Read the second paragraph and separate the pieces of information.

1. _____

2. _____

3. _____

2 In very hot countries, why do frogs need to aestivate? [2]

Look out for the word aestivate – the answer will be nearby.

_____
_____

3 Which of these problems might stop a hedgehog from surviving the winter? Mark each problem as true or false. The first one has been done for you. [2]

	True	False
Their nest is not comfortable enough.		✓
They do not like rabbit holes.		
They might wake up too soon.		
They do not like cat or dog food.		

4 '… *rising temperature signals that* …'
Circle the word in the list below that is closest in meaning to *signals*. [1]

Try the words in the phrase and check it makes sense.

lights   calls   shows   flushes

© Pearson Education Limited 2018   *Pinpoint English Comprehension Year 4*   79

Unit 15

Name _____

Class _____

1 '*When food is scarce …*'
What does *scarce* tell you about the food? Tick **one** box. [1]

The food is too cold. ☐   It makes them sleepy. ☐

There is not much food. ☐   It is in scary places. ☐

2 What **two** purposes does this text have? [2]

Think about what you have learned from this text.

1. _____

2. _____

3 a) What is the difference between hibernation and aestivation? [1]

_____

b) What are the similarities? [1]

_____

4 Why is it a bad idea for a ladybird to hibernate in a house? [2]

Think carefully about the whole text.

_____

_____

_____

5 Why is this text called *Sleeping for Survival*? [1]

_____

_____

The Secret Garden

An excerpt adapted from the original by Frances Hodgson Burnett

Mary is sent to live with her uncle following the death of her parents. She is enjoying spending time exploring the gardens surrounding her uncle's house.

Mary had begun to like the garden, and she had begun to like the robin. She had begun to like Dickon, Martha, and Martha's mother, too. That seemed a lot of people to like when you were not used to liking people. She walked next to the long, ivy-covered wall, looking up at the treetops that peeped over it. When she walked back again the most interesting thing happened to her and all because of the robin.

She heard a chirp and a twitter and there he was, just hopping about. He was trying to pretend that he had not followed her, but she knew he had. The surprise made her shiver with happiness.

"You do remember me!" she cried out. "You do! You are prettier than anything else in the world!"

She chirped, and talked, and coaxed him. He hopped and flirted his tail and twittered. It was as if he were talking to her, too. His red waistcoat was like satin as he puffed out his tiny breast. It was like he wanted her to know how like a man a robin could be. Mary forgot that she had ever been unfriendly in her life, and the robin let her get closer and closer to him.

> To *coax someone*, is to gently persuade them to do something.

Oh! How nice that he should let her come so close. Mary felt that the robin knew she would never scare him, and that he knew it because he was a real person, nicer than any other person in the world. Mary was so happy that she didn't even want to breathe.

She saw the robin hop over a small pile of earth where the dog had scratched a deep hole, trying to dig up a mole. As Mary looked at the hole, she saw something half buried in the soil. It looked like a ring of rusty iron or brass. So she put out her hand and picked it up. It was more than a ring, it was an old key. It looked as if it had been buried for a long time.

Unit 16

The Secret Garden

"Maybe it has been buried for ten years," Mary said in a whisper. "Maybe it is the key to the garden!" She looked almost scared.

Mary had heard a lot about magic in her ayah's stories. She always said that what happened next was magic.

An *ayah* is an Indian nanny.

Little gusts of wind rushed down the walk. One gust was stronger than the rest, strong enough to wave the branches of the trees, and strong enough to blow the ivy hanging from the wall and push away some loose stems. Mary saw something under the ivy. It was a round knob. It was the knob of a door.

Name _____

Class _____

Unit 16

1 At the beginning of the extract, what is Mary not used to? Tick **one** box. [1]

liking robins ☐   liking Martha's mother ☐

liking gardens ☐   liking people ☐

2 Mark each description of the robin as true or false. The first one has been done for you. [2]

Read the text carefully.

	True	False
He is wearing a red waistcoat.		✓
He hops and twitters.		
He talks like a man.		
He puffs up his chest.		

3 Number these main events 1-6 to put them in the correct order. The first one has been done for you. [1]

Mary talks to the robin. ☐   Mary walks next to a wall. ☐ 1

Mary sees a doorknob. ☐   The robin hops over a pile of earth. ☐

Mary hears the robin. ☐   Mary finds a key. ☐

4 **Find** and **copy two** separate words that are bird noises. [2]

Read the second paragraph again.

1. _____

2. _____

© Pearson Education Limited 2018   Pinpoint English Comprehension Year 4   83

Unit 16

Name _____

Class _____

1 *'Mary had begun to like the garden, and she had begun to like the robin.'*

What does this tell you about how Mary used to feel? [1]

_____

2 *'… the treetops peeped over it.'*

What does *peeped* tell you about the trees? Tick **one** box. [1]

They are magical. ☐

They are only a bit taller than the wall. ☐

They are covered in ivy. ☐

3 *'It looked like it had been buried for a long time.'*

What is *it*? How does it look like it had been buried for a long time? [2]

Remember to answer both parts.

_____

_____

4 *' … the most interesting thing happened to her …'*

What was the *most interesting thing*? Tick **one** box. [1]

starting to like people ☐   finding the key and the door ☐

making friends with the robin ☐   forgetting she used to be nasty ☐

Name _____

Class _____

Unit 16

1. How do you know that Mary was unfriendly once? [2]

_____

_____

2. **Find** and **copy** a **group of words** that tell you Mary is *incredibly happy*. [1]

_____

3. '*"Maybe it has been buried for ten years," Mary said in a whisper.*'

Mark each explanation of why she might be whispering as true or false. Tick the correct box. [2]

Imagine how she is feeling.

	True	False
She feels a bit nervous.		
The key is mysterious.		
She might scare the robin.		
She wants to keep the garden secret.		

4. '*She always said that what happened next was magic.*'
What happened, and why did she think it was magic? [2]

_____

_____

5. What led Mary to find the key? [2]

_____

_____

© Pearson Education Limited 2018 — Pinpoint English Comprehension Year 4

Unit 17: Who Has Seen the Wind? *and* Hurt No Living Thing

By Christina Rossetti

Who Has Seen the Wind?

Who has seen the wind?
Neither I nor you:
But when the leaves hang trembling,
The wind is passing through.

Who has seen the wind?
Neither you nor I:
But when the trees bow down their heads,
The wind is passing by.

Hurt No Living Thing

Hurt no living thing:
Ladybird, nor butterfly,
Nor moth with dusty wing,
Nor cricket chirping cheerily,
Nor grasshopper so light of leap,
Nor dancing gnat, nor beetle fat,
Nor harmless worms that creep.

Name _____

Class _____

Unit **17**

1 Look at *Who Has Seen the Wind?*. Mark each description of the poem as true or false. The first one has been done for you. [2]

Re-read the poem a number of times.

	True	False
Nobody sees the wind but we see what it does.	✓	
Trees can see the wind.		
You and I can't see the wind but the trees show us it is there.		
You and I should tremble and bow to the wind.		

2 **Find** and **copy one** word that means *shaking*. [1]

_____

3 Look at *Hurt No Living Thing*. Draw a line to match the creature to its description. The first one has been done for you. [1]

Read each line of the poem carefully.

Creature	Description
cricket	dancing
moth	light of leap
grasshopper	chirping cheerily
gnat	harmless
beetle	dusty wing
worms	fat

© Pearson Education Limited 2018 — *Pinpoint English Comprehension Year 4*

Unit 17

Name _____

Class _____

1 In *Who Has Seen the Wind?* how does the strength of the wind differ in the first and second verses? Give evidence for your answers. [2]

Think about what the wind does to the trees.

_____

_____

2 Why has the poet chosen to write only about very small creatures in *Hurt No Living Thing*? Mark each explanation as true or false. The first one has been done for you. [2]

	True	False
They are more likely to be hurt.	✓	
We must not forget they are animals too.		
She thinks they are really cute.		
Little creatures are more important.		

3 Look at *Hurt No Living Thing*. **Find** and **copy one** word that is closest in meaning to *happily*. [1]

_____

4 Look at *Hurt No Living Thing*. Why might the poet have chosen to describe the creatures' details? Tick **two** boxes. [2]

To show that they all have different characteristics. ☐

To help you decide which one is the best. ☐

To show which one she likes the best. ☐

To make you notice their special qualities. ☐

Name _____

Class _____

Unit 17

1. In *Who Has Seen the Wind?* what is the effect of the repetition in the first two lines of each verse? Tick **one** box. [1]

   It makes you wonder about the wind. ☐

   It emphasises that no one sees the wind. ☐

   It gives a varied rhythm. ☐

   It makes it more puzzling. ☐

2. In *Hurt No Living Thing* what is the effect of listing little living things? [2]

   _____
   _____

   Think about the poem as a whole and how it makes you feel.

3. Look at *Hurt No Living Thing*. **Find** and **copy** the **group of words** that describes how an animal jumps? [1]

   _____

4. What do the two poems tell you about the poet? [2]

   _____
   _____
   _____
   _____

   What do the poems have in common? Remember to make your answer about the poet.

Unit 18: Mount Everest

At over 8,800 metres tall, Mount Everest is the tallest mountain in the world. It is part of a mountain range called the Himalayas. This range crosses several countries in Asia including India, Pakistan and China. The ten tallest mountains in the world are all in this area.

Mountain	Height
Mount Everest	8,848 m
K2	8,611 m
Kangchenjunga	8,586 m
Lhotse	8,516 m
Makalu	8,485 m
Cho Oyu	8,188 m
Dhaulagiri	8,167 m
Manaslu	8,163 m
Nanga Parbat	8,126 m
Annapurna	8,091 m

People are very interested in this amazing mountain. Some people try to climb to the summit but it is not an easy task. There is not much oxygen up there and people have to adjust to the low oxygen levels.

The *summit* is the very top of a mountain.

Everest Fact!

Mount Everest was formed sixty million years ago and it is still growing – it grows about five centimetres every year.

Climbers start at a base camp where they rest and prepare their supplies. There are more camps on the way up to the top of the mountain. Climbers rest at each one to let their bodies adjust to the altitude.

The *altitude* is how high up something is.

Unit 18

Everest Fact!

The first person to climb to the top of Mount Everest was Sir Edmund Hillary. He reached the summit in 1955.

The summit of Mount Everest is covered with dazzling, deep snow all year round. It is very cold and windy up there and this makes the climb very risky. Climbers have special gear including ice axes, special boots and clothing, sunglasses and radios to help them stay safe on their journey.

Sherpas

Sherpas are local people who know Mount Everest well. They are famous for their mountaineering skills. Sherpas guide visitors who are climbing the mountain and can help the climbers by transporting things up the mountain for them on yaks.

> A *yak* is a species of cattle. It is strong, with a thick, shaggy coat.

Reaching the summit of Mount Everest is an amazing achievement. Not many people have ever done it. Sadly, not everyone survives the trek up Mount Everest. More than 250 people have died while climbing the mountain. This sad fact reminds us of the dangers of the challenge.

Unit 18

Name _____

Class _____

1 What is the name of the mountain range in which Mount Everest is found? [1]

_____

2 List the **three** tallest mountains after Mount Everest. [3]

1. _____

2. _____

3. _____

3 Mark each fact about Mount Everest as true or false. The first one has been done for you. [2]

The answers are in the Everest Fact! boxes and the table.

	True	False
Everest grows exactly 5 cm a year.		✓
Everest formed 60 million years ago.		
Everest stays the same size.		
Everest is currently 8,848 m tall.		
Everest shrinks about 5 cm a year.		

4 Sir Edmund Hillary reached the top of Mount Everest in 1955. Why is this important and remembered? Tick **one** box. [1]

He started at the base camp. ☐

He was the first person to reach the summit. ☐

He discovered Mount Everest. ☐

Nobody else had climbed Mount Everest. ☐

The answer is in the first paragraph.

Name _____

Class _____

Unit 18

1. Find one difficulty mentioned in the text that makes climbing Mount Everest not an easy task. [1]

   Look for an explanation for the fact that it is not an easy task.

   _____

2. Look at the table. Why have these mountains been chosen to go into the table? [1]

   _____
   _____

3. 'Climbers rest ... to let their bodies adjust to the altitude.'
   Which of the definitions below is closest in meaning to *adjust* as it is used here? Tick **one** box. [1]

   climbing up ☐   get used to ☐

   lower themselves ☐   breathe in ☐

4. Find **two** things that climbers do at camps on Mount Everest. [2]

   Look at what the climbers do at the base camp first.

   1. _____
   2. _____

5. 'The summit of Mount Everest is covered in dazzling, deep snow all year round.'
   Explain why *sunglasses* are included in the list of special gear to protect climbers. [1]

   _____

Unit 18   D

Name _____

Class _____

1 *'Climbing up Mount Everest is an amazing feat.'*

Which of the following is closest in meaning to *an amazing feat* as it is used in this sentence? Tick **one** box. [1]

> Swap the definitions in to the sentence and check that it still makes sense.

an achievement that requires great courage, skill and strength ☐

an incredible distance to travel upwards ☐

a completely unrealistic thing to do ☐

a strongly competitive feature of most climbs ☐

2 *'More than 250 people have died while climbing the mountain.'*

Why is this information included in the text? [2]

> Think about what this sentence adds to your understanding of Mount Everest.

_____

_____

3 Look at the section headed *Sherpas*.

a) Give **two** reasons why Sherpas make such excellent guides for visitors and climbers. [2]

_____

_____

b) How else do Sherpas help climbers? [1]

_____

94   © Pearson Education Limited 2018   *Pinpoint English Comprehension Year 4*

Making Room for Bikes

January 20

Dear Mayor,

I am writing to inform you of a serious problem affecting our town. There are no safe routes for people to ride bikes. This issue has been brought to my attention following an incident involving my family and I last Thursday. I was enjoying a pleasant cycle ride home from school with my mum and my sister. We were riding our bikes along Holloway Drive when, all of a sudden, a large vehicle pulled out right in front of us. We were forced to slam on our brakes and my younger sister actually fell from her bike. The driver didn't even stop. He drove off and continued with his journey.

We were cycling as safely as possible: riding on the left-hand side of the road, wearing hi-visibility jackets and helmets, and we all had reflective lights on our bikes. Had we not been able to stop so quickly, I fear the outcome would have been much more serious. I worry that very soon someone may be badly injured, or worse.

Many other towns have created cycle paths and cycle lanes, and have signs to warn drivers that cyclists are also using the roads. I think this is something that we need in Great Wittledon. In addition, I think it would help if the speed limit in and around the town was reduced from 30 mph to 20 mph.

I realise that these changes will cost the local council money, but can you really put a price on someone's life?

I appreciate you taking the time to consider my concerns. I hope you agree that the changes suggested in this letter will greatly benefit everyone in Great Wittledon.

Yours sincerely,

Josh Parker

Unit 19

Name _____

Class _____

1. Number the events of the incident 1-5 in order. The first one has been done for you. [1]

   They slammed on the brakes. ☐

   The driver continued his journey. ☐

   They were enjoying a pleasant bicycle ride home. ☐ 1

   The sister fell off her bike. ☐

   A large vehicle pulled out in front of them. ☐

2. Who was the letter-writer with when the incident happened? [1]

   The answer is in the first paragraph.

   _____

3. Give **two** things the letter-writer says he and his family were doing to cycle safely. [2]

   1. _____

   2. _____

4. Mark each fact about where the accident happened as true or false. The first one has been done for you. [2]

   Re-read the first three paragraphs again.

	True	False
on the way home from school	✓	
on a cycle path		
on Holloway Drive		
in Great Wittledon		

Name _____

Class _____

Unit 19

1 What is the serious problem affecting the town, according to the letter-writer? Tick **one** box. [1]

His family had an incident. ☐

There are no safe spaces for people to ride bikes. ☐

His younger sister fell off her bike. ☐

It happened on Thursday. ☐

2 a) Find **two** things the letter-writer says other towns have done to improve cycling safety? [2]

1. _____

2. _____

b) What additional safety suggestion do they make? [1]

_____

3 **Find** and **copy one** word that tells you that the Parker family had to use their bicycle brakes very *quickly* and *powerfully*. [1]

_____

4 a) Who is the letter-writer writing to? [1]

_____

Think about who is he trying to help.

b) As well as his family, who is he writing the letter for? [1]

_____

Unit 19

Name _____

Class _____

1 *'This issue has been brought to my attention ...'*
Which of the following is closest in meaning to *brought to my attention*? Tick **one** box. [1]

It has been terrifying me. ☐

They have been knocking me over. ☐

Cars are hurting cyclists. ☐

I have noticed it. ☐

2 What clues are there that the Parker family had good brakes on their bicycles? [2]

The clues are in two paragraphs.

_____
_____

3 *'... can you really put a price on someone's life?'*
Why does the letter-writer say this? [2]

It is important to understand this sentence and the sentence before it.

_____
_____

4 What is the purpose of Josh's letter to the Mayor? [3]

_____
_____
_____

The Lion's Share

Unit 20

This story is one of Aesop's fables.

One day, a lion, a fox, a jackal and a wolf went hunting together. They were unlikely companions, but all of them were hungry and all realised that they had more chance of a decent meal if they worked together to find one. They hunted all morning but they could not find anything satisfactory. It was only in the late afternoon that they finally caught a deer. The four beasts surrounded the poor animal and killed it as quickly as they could. Then it was time to decide how to share their food.

A *fable* is a short story which usually has animals as characters. Fables always have a moral, or a lesson, at the end.

The mighty lion was the Lord of the Jungle. He had eyes of gold, fur of velvet and claws of steel. He was superior to all the other animals in strength.

Carcass means the dead body of an animal.

So the other creatures agreed when he proposed to divide the food into four portions. Placing one of his paws upon the carcass of the deer, the lion said, "You see, as the Lord of the Jungle, it is my right to receive a portion of any meat that has come from my domain."

Domain means an area that someone rules.

Unit 20

The Lion's Share

The fox, the jackal and the wolf nodded in agreement.

"I am also the King of Beasts, so I must receive another portion for my royal household," declared the lion, staring unflinchingly at the other animals.

They looked at each other uneasily. Before any of them could respond the lion spoke again.

"And besides, I was leading the hunt, so I deserve a third portion for my successful hunting strategy," he proclaimed.

> A *strategy* is a plan for achieving something.

The others mumbled something, but it could not be heard.

"As for the fourth portion, if you wish to discuss its ownership, let's begin, and we will see who will get it," continued the lion, stretching his claws absent-mindedly.

"Humph," the others grumbled. They walked away with their heads down.

They knew it was pointless to argue with the lion about their shares.

The moral of this story is: You may work hard to help to achieve something but you won't always receive the reward.

Name _____

Class _____

Unit 20

1. How many animals went hunting together? [1]

   _____

2. Number the events of the incident 1–5 in order. The first one has been done for you. [1]

   The animals agree to work together. ☐

   The animals feel hungry. [1]

   The fox, jackal and wolf grumble and walk off. ☐

   They catch deer in the late afternoon. ☐

   The lion explains why he should get three portions. ☐

   Make sure you read the whole text before answering.

3. 'It was only in the late afternoon that they finally caught a deer.'

   What does *finally* tell you about their hunt? Tick **one** box. [1]

   It was the lion's idea. ☐

   They had worked together. ☐

   They had nearly finished. ☐

   It took a long time. ☐

   Re-read this sentence and the one before.

4. How is the appearance of the lion described? [1]

   _____

   _____

Unit 20

Name _____

Class _____

1 Why were the animals hunting together? Give **two** reasons. [2]

1. _____

2. _____

2 '*The others mumbled something, but it could not be heard.*'

Why do you think they did not argue with the lion? [1]

> Think about how the animals were feeling as the lion spoke!

_____

_____

3 **Find** and **copy one** word which has a similar meaning to *prize*. [1]

_____

4 Which of the following would make the best replacement title for the story? Tick **one** box. [1]

The Poor Deer	☐
The Happy Hunters	☐
The Fairest One	☐
The Selfish King	☐

102 © Pearson Education Limited 2018 — Pinpoint English Comprehension Year 4

Name _____

Class _____

Unit 20

1 a) Whose idea was it to divide the deer into four parts? [1]

_____

b) Why did the other animals *nod in agreement* at first? [1]

_____

2 '*... declared the lion, staring unflinchingly.*'
What does *unflinchingly* suggest about the way that the lion stared? Tick **one** box. [1]

> Think about the lion's character!

nervously ☐   feeling guilty ☐

unsurely ☐   without any fear ☐

3 Describe the personality of the lion as fully as you can, drawing on what he says and does. Give at least **two** pieces of evidence. [3]

_____
_____
_____
_____

4 Do you think the other animals will hunt with the lion again? Explain your answer based on your understanding of the text. Complete the sentence below. [1]

_____ because _____
_____
_____

Unit 1

Answers: The Life of Amelia Earhart

LEVEL: Towards	
❶ Mark the statement about Amelia Earhart as a child as true or false. [2]	
Answer: False (given); True; False; True *Award one mark for two correct answers; two marks for three correct answers.*	
Content domain reference	2b
Comprehension strategies	Retrieving and recording information; Recall
❷ Draw lines to match the years to the facts about Amelia Earhart. [2]	
Answer: 1897 – was born (given) 1921 – first flying lesson 1932 – first solo flight across the Atlantic 1935 – flew across the Pacific 1937 – left the USA in the *Electra* *Award one mark for two or three correct answers; two marks for all four.*	
Content domain reference	2b
Comprehension strategies	Retrieving and recording information; Clarifying
❸ **Find** and **copy one** word in the *Flying Fact!* section that tells you Amelia flew *alone*. [1]	
Answer: solo	
Content domain reference	2a
Comprehension strategies	Giving meaning of words in context; Making inferences
❹ What were the **two** jobs that Amelia Earhart did to help her save up for her first plane? [2]	
Answer: nursing assistant; social worker	
Content domain reference	2b
Comprehension strategies	Retrieving and recording information
LEVEL: Securing	
❶ Number the list of events from Amelia Earhart's life 1-5 to put them in the right order. [1]	
Answer: She flew from Canada to Ireland. (3); She had flying lessons. (1) (given); She set off in the *Electra* to fly around the world. (5); She flew across the Pacific Ocean alone. (4); She became the first woman to cross the Atlantic in a plane. (2)	
Content domain reference	2c
Comprehension strategies	Retrieving and recording information; Summarising
❷ What does *instantly hooked* tell you about her attitude to flying? Tick **one** box. [1]	
Answer: immediately gripped	
Content domain reference	2a
Comprehension strategies	Giving meaning of words in context; Clarifying
❸ According to the text, what **two** records did Amelia Earhart break before 1932? [2]	
Answer: flew to an altitude of 4,270 metres; first woman to cross Atlantic in a plane	
Content domain reference	2b
Comprehension strategies	Clarifying; Retrieving and recording information

🖉 Which of the below best matches the meaning of *tackle*? [1]	
Answer: get to grips with	
Content domain reference	2a
Comprehension strategies	Giving meaning of words in context; Making inferences
LEVEL: Deeper	
🖉 In this text, two of Amelia Earhart's planes are named: one is her first plane, and one is her last. Finish these sentences by adding in the names, and explaining how you know which is which. [2]	
Answer: *Award one mark for: Canary* – she saved her money to buy it.; She learned a lot about flying in it.; She bought it shortly after her first flying lesson. *Award one mark for: Electra* – She was in it when she disappeared.	
Content domain reference	2h
Comprehension strategies	Making comparisons within the text; Making connections
🖉 What problems and obstacles did Amelia Earhart face as a pilot? Use the whole text to give **three** examples. [3]	
Answer: *Award one mark for each answer similar to:* She had to save and buy her first plane.; She wasn't allowed to fly across the Atlantic because she was a woman.; She experienced bad weather (when trying to break records).	
Content domain reference	2c
Comprehension strategies	Summarising; Retrieving and recording information
🖉 Find examples from throughout Amelia Earhart's life of her independence and determination. [3]	
Answer: *Award one mark for each answer similar to:* She worked and saved for her first plane.; She set flying records.; being a passenger was not enough – wanted to fly herself; She wanted to do it alone.; She attempted to be the first woman to fly around the world – and almost made it.	
Content domain reference	2b/d
Comprehension strategies	Making inferences; Retrieving and recording information
🖉 'Experts are still trying to solve the mystery …' Why is it still a *mystery*? [1]	
Answer: *Award one mark for answers similar to:* She was never seen again.; Her radio just went silent and there was no explanation.; No one has found her or her plane.	
Content domain reference	2b/d
Comprehension strategies	Making inferences; Clarifying

Unit 2

Answers: Hitting the Slopes

LEVEL: Towards	
1 According to the text, what can top skiers and snowboarders both do? [1]	
Answer: tricks, jumps and spins	
Content domain reference	2b
Comprehension strategies	Retrieving and recording information; Recall
2 Draw lines to match the equipment to the sport, as described in the text. [1]	
Answer: Skiing: two long plastic strips; sticks for balance Snowboarding: flat board; special boots	
Content domain reference	2b
Comprehension strategies	Retrieving and recording information; Clarifying
3 Give **two** things you can learn about *snurfing* from this text. [2]	
Answer: *Award one mark for each answer similar to:* invented by a skier; two skis; a rope to steer; The name is a cross between snow and surf.; There were snurfing competitions.	
Content domain reference	2b
Comprehension strategies	Retrieving and recording information; Recall
4 Find and **copy** the **group of words** that tells you more and more people liked the sport of snowboarding. [1]	
Answer: gained popularity	
Content domain reference	2a
Comprehension strategies	Giving meaning of words in context; Clarifying
5 Mark each fact as true or false. [2]	
Answer: False (given); True; True; False *Award one mark for two correct answers; two marks for three correct answers.*	
Content domain reference	2b/d
Comprehension strategies	Retrieving and recording information; Making inferences
LEVEL: Securing	
1 What did people add to their boards to make jumps and tricks possible for snurfers? [1]	
Answer: flexible straps	
Content domain reference	2b
Comprehension strategies	Retrieving and recording information; Clarifying
2 Mark the statements about the length of snowboards as true or false. [2]	
Answer: False (given); True; True; False *Award one mark for two correct answers; two marks for three correct answers.*	
Content domain reference	2b/d
Comprehension strategies	Retrieving and recording information; Clarifying

3 '*Attitudes gradually began to change …*' What does this tell you about skiers' views on snowboarding? [2]	
Answer: *Award one mark for each answer similar to:* They slowly accepted it.; They accepted it but it took a while.; They didn't ban snowboarding forever.	
Content domain reference	2b
Comprehension strategies	Retrieving and recording information; Making inferences
4 **Find** and **copy one** word that tells you the sport grabbed people's attention. [1]	
Answer: captivated	
Content domain reference	2a
Comprehension strategies	Giving meaning of words in context; Clarifying
LEVEL: Deeper	
1 Why did few ski centres allow snowboarders on their runs, at first? Identify two reasons by ticking **two** statements below. [2]	
Answer: In case snowboarders ruined their ski runs.; They were worried snow would be swept off by the boards.	
Content domain reference	2b
Comprehension strategies	Retrieving and recording information; Clarifying
2 Why are the somersaults and spins of top athletes described as *breathtaking*? [2]	
Answer: *Award two marks for answers similar to:* They are so astonishing/remarkable/amazing/awesome that people watching gasp or their breath is taken away.	
Content domain reference	2g
Comprehension strategies	Identifying/explaining how meaning is enhanced by choice of words and phrases
3 From your reading of the whole text, which of the titles below would make a good alternative to *Hitting the Slopes*? [1]	
Answer: The Birth and Growth of Snowboarding	
Content domain reference	2c
Comprehension strategies	Making connections
4 How has snowboarding changed since the 1920s? Give **three** ways using evidence from across the text. [3]	
Answer: *Award up to three marks for points that give the sense of an evolution towards increased acceptance/popularity, similar to:* When it began, it was just wood tied to your feet using horse reins.; In 1965, the snurfboard was invented and it was made of two skis tied together plus a rope for steering.; In the 1970s, flexible straps were added for doing tricks.; At first, it wasn't easy to find somewhere to snowboard.; It was gradually accepted to become one of the most popular sports and it still is.; Designs got better and better especially in the 1980s.; It entered the Olympics in 1998 and the spectacle of it made the sport very popular.	
Content domain reference	2h
Comprehension strategies	Making comparisons within the text

Unit 3

Answers: School Tomorrow – Excuses for Mum

LEVEL: Towards	
❶ Look at the verse which begins, '*I can't go to school tomorrow …*'. What is this verse all about? [1]	
Answer: The character is too ill to go to school.	
Content domain reference	2c
Comprehension strategies	Summarising
❷ Mark these statements about the whole poem as true or false [2]	
Answer: False (given); True; False; True *Award one mark for two correct answers; two marks for three correct answers.*	
Content domain reference	2d
Comprehension strategies	Making inferences; Summarising
❸ **Find** and **copy one** word in the verse beginning *I'll stay home and clean and cook* that means the same as *deal with*. [1]	
Answer: handle	
Content domain reference	2a
Comprehension strategies	Giving meaning of words in context
❹ List **three** things the boy realises that he will miss if he doesn't go to school. [3]	
Answer: *Award one mark for each answer similar to:* friends; Romans topic; results; laughing in assembly; joking with Mr Lindon; playing football; making a circuit; quoting Shakespeare	
Content domain reference	2b
Comprehension strategies	Retrieving and recording information; Clarifying
LEVEL: Securing	
❶ Draw lines to show which of these excuses that the boy makes are realistic, and which are unrealistic. [2]	
Answer: Realistic: My uniform is dirty.; I'm sick. (given); I haven't done my homework. Unrealistic: I have the plague. (given); The school ran away.; I'll pay the bills. *Award one mark for two or three correct answers; two marks for all four correct.*	
Content domain reference	2d
Comprehension strategies	Making inferences; Clarifying
❷ What feeling is the poet suggesting with the use of an exclamation mark here? [1]	
Answer: *Acceptable answers include:* to show his sudden awareness/horror/shock/disappointment *Do not accept:* shouting, as this is not a feeling.	
Content domain reference	2g
Comprehension strategies	Identifying/explaining how meaning is enhanced by choice of words and phrases; Making inferences

Unit 3

3	What is the effect of having so many excuses listed together? Mark the answers as true or false [2]
Answer:	True (given); False; True; True; False
	Award one mark for two or three correct answers; two marks for all four correct.
Content domain reference	2f
Comprehension strategies	Clarifying; Making connections; Identifying/explaining how meaning is enhanced by choice of words and phrases

LEVEL: Deeper	
1	In the final verse, what does the boy realise about staying at home? Give **two** things and support your answer with details from the poem. [3]
Answer:	*Award up to three marks for answers that refer to both parts and include evidence similar to:*
	Staying at home isn't easy - it involves work: getting shopping, paying bills, cleaning and cooking.; He'll miss all the fun of school: football, friends, jokes and different things to learn about - circuits, Romans, Shakespeare.
Content domain reference	2d
Comprehension strategies	Making inferences; Summarising
2	What is this poem about? Tick **one** answer from the list below. [1]
Answer:	A boy who realises he likes school.
Content domain reference	2c
Comprehension strategies	Summarising; Making inferences
3	Why might this poem be seen as funny by many people? Try to explain in detail. [3]
Answer:	*Award three marks for answers similar to:*
	It has many silly excuses.; Some of the excuses are very extreme.; Some of the reasons are familiar/the sort of things people do say.; It feels familiar (end of the holidays).; Some of the excuses sound a bit like an adult speaking.; The repetitive excuses sound funny.
	Accept any unique/reasonable answer.
Content domain reference	2f
Comprehension strategies	Summarising; Evaluating; Making inferences; Making connections

Unit 4

Answers: The Jungle Book

LEVEL: Towards	
❶ What made Rikki-tikki feel proud? Tick **one** box. [1]	
Answer: his jumping skills	
Content domain reference	2b
Comprehension strategies	Retrieving and recording information; Making connections
❷ '"Be careful. I am Death!"' Who says this in the story? [1]	
Answer: the karait; the snake	
Content domain reference	2b
Comprehension strategies	Retrieving and recording information; Clarifying
❸ Why was the karait a real danger? Mark the answers as true or false. [2]	
Answer: True (given); True; False; False; True *Award one mark for two or three correct answers; two marks for all four correct.*	
Content domain reference	2b
Comprehension strategies	Retrieving and recording information; Clarifying
❹ 'But just as Teddy was stooping …' Which of the words below is closest in meaning to *stooping*? Tick **one** box. [1]	
Answer: bending	
Content domain reference	2a
Comprehension strategies	Giving meaning of words in context; Clarifying
LEVEL: Securing	
❶ What does the word *lashed* tell you about the way in which the snake moved? Tick **one** box. [1]	
Answer: suddenly and violently	
Content domain reference	2g
Comprehension strategies	Giving meaning of words in context; Identifying/explaining how meaning is enhanced by choice of words and phrases
❷ Give **two** reasons why Rikki-tikki is important to the family. [2]	
Answer: He protects them (from snakes).; He is a pet for Teddy; Teddy likes stroking/petting him.	
Content domain reference	2d
Comprehension strategies	Retrieving and recording information; Making inferences
❸ Draw lines to match the character to what they do in the battle between snake and mongoose. [2]	
Answer: Teddy – calls to parents (given) Mother – cries out in a piercing way Father – rushes with stick to attack snake Mongoose – jumps on enemy's back Snake – lunges too far *Award one mark for two or three correct answers; two marks for all four correct.*	
Content domain reference	2b/d
Comprehension strategies	Retrieving and recording information; Making inferences; Clarifying

Unit 4

⚡ '*A full meal makes a slow mongoose.*' How does this statement explain Rikki-tikki's actions at the end of the fight? [2]	
Answer: *Award one mark for:* He decides not to eat the snake. *Award two marks for:* He doesn't eat the snake because being full will make him slow/less good at fighting snakes.	
Content domain reference	2d
Comprehension strategies	Retrieving and recording information; Recall; Making inferences
LEVEL: Deeper	
⚡ a) How do mongooses win fights with snakes in the old books? [1] b) How do mongooses win fights with snakes in this story? [1]	
Answer: a) After a fight, the mongoose eats herbs that cure him of the poisonous bite. b) A mongoose is so fast that it isn't bitten during a fight.	
Content domain reference	2b
Comprehension strategies	Retrieving and recording information; Clarifying
⚡ '*… the mongoose has a jump that is more wonderful than a magical herb.*' What does this tell you about the jump of a mongoose? Mark each answer as true or false [2]	
Answer: True (given); False; False; True *Award one mark for two correct answers; two marks for three correct answers.*	
Content domain reference	2g
Comprehension strategies	Identifying/explaining how meaning is enhanced by choice of words and phrases; Making inferences; Clarifying
⚡ How does the author make you realise just how dangerous the fight with the karait was for Rikki-tikki? Give examples from the text. [3]	
Answer: *Award three marks for answers similar to:* Shows how close the karait got: '… within a fraction of his shoulder' ; '…the snake's head followed his heels closely'; ' Rikki did not know that fighting the karait was much more dangerous than fighting the cobra …'; ' … bite as deadly as the cobra's …' *Accept any unique/reasonable answer.*	
Content domain reference	2f
Comprehension strategies	Making connections; Making inferences; Clarifying

Unit 5

Answers: Monarch Butterflies

LEVEL: Towards	
1 How can you tell the difference between a male and female Monarch butterfly? [1]	
Answer: The male has a black spot on its wings and the female doesn't.	
Content domain reference	2b
Comprehension strategies	Retrieving and recording information; Clarifying
2 According to the text, what do the bright wings of the Monarch do? Tick **one** box. [1]	
Answer: tell predators that the butterfly is poisonous	
Content domain reference	2b
Comprehension strategies	Retrieving and recording information; Clarifying
3 How is the Monarch different from other butterflies? [1]	
Answer: It flaps its wings more slowly.	
Content domain reference	2b
Comprehension strategies	Retrieving and recording information; Recall
4 What other names do people give the Monarch butterfly? Find **three** names. [1]	
Answer: King Billy; Milkweed butterflies; wanderers	
Content domain reference	2b
Comprehension strategies	Retrieving and recording information; Recall
5 Look at the *Life cycle of a Monarch butterfly*. **Find** and **copy one** word that means the same as *comes out*. [1]	
Answer: emerges	
Content domain reference	2a
Comprehension strategies	Giving meaning of words in context; Retrieving and recording information
LEVEL: Securing	
1 What does the word *striking* tell you about their wings? Tick **one** box. [1]	
Answer: they are eye-catching	
Content domain reference	2a
Comprehension strategies	Giving meaning of words in context
2 Find **two** facts that tell you about the rapid growth of the caterpillar. [2]	
Answer: *Award one mark for each answer similar to:* They can eat a whole leaf in five minutes.; They gain about 2700 times their weight.; The caterpillar sheds its skin 5 times.	
Content domain reference	2b
Comprehension strategies	Retrieving and recording information; Clarifying
3 Mark these statements about milkweed plants as true or false. [2]	
Answer: True (given); False; True; False *Award one mark for two correct answers; two marks for three correct answers.*	
Content domain reference	2b
Comprehension strategies	Retrieving and recording information; Clarifying

Unit 5

🔑 Number these facts about the caterpillar 1–4 in the correct order. [1]	
Answer: attaches itself to a branch with silk (2); leaves the chrysalis as a butterfly (4); sheds its skin 5 times (1) (given); forms a chrysalis (3)	
Content domain reference	2c
Comprehension strategies	Summarising; Retrieving and recording information
LEVEL: Deeper	
🔑 a) Which word best describes the author's view of Monarch butterflies? Circle **one**. [1] b) Explain your answer, giving evidence from the text. [2]	
Answer: a) special b) *Award one mark for each answer similar to:* They are described as stunning creatures, with striking patterns.; Even their colours are special as they are used to protect them rather than to attract predators.; They aren't killed by the milkweed poison. *Accept any unique/reasonable answer.*	
Content domain reference	2f
Comprehension strategies	Making inferences; Identifying/explaining how meaning is enhanced by choice of words and phrases; Making connections
🔑 What does *huge swarm* tell you about the way that Monarch butterflies migrate? [1]	
Answer: They fly in very large numbers as a group/crowd/close together.	
Content domain reference	2a
Comprehension strategies	Giving meaning of words in context; Clarifying
🔑 Draw lines to match the facts to the time when Monarch butterflies emerge. [2]	
Answer: spring and summer: lay eggs on milkweed plant (given); live between two and six weeks autumn: live between six and eight months; travel in huge swarms; migrate to warmer places; lay eggs on milkweed plant *Award one mark for three or four correct answers; two marks for all five correct.*	
Content domain reference	2b
Comprehension strategies	Retrieving and recording information; Clarifying

Unit 6

Answers: Heartsong

LEVEL: Towards	
❓ With what does the narrator compare the noise she makes with the viola? Tick **one** box. [1]	
Answer: a donkey	
Content domain reference	2b
Comprehension strategies	Retrieving and recording information; Clarifying
❓ What job does Father Antonio do? Tick **one** box. [1]	
Answer: music master	
Content domain reference	2d
Comprehension strategies	Making inferences; Clarifying
❓ What is the narrator's name, and how do you know? [2]	
Answer: Laura Father Antonio calls her Laura. *Award one mark for each answer.*	
Content domain reference	2d
Comprehension strategies	Making inferences; Retrieving and recording information; Clarifying
❓ Number these events from the story 1–4 in the correct order. [1]	
Answer: She plays the viola badly. (1) (given); The sister joins in the fun. (3); Father Antonio laughs. (2); Father Antonio gives her a flute. (4)	
Content domain reference	2c
Comprehension strategies	Summarising; Making inferences; Identifying/explaining how meaning is enhanced by choice of words and phrases
LEVEL: Securing	
❓ '*Father Antonio winced as if he were sucking a lemon, but then he laughed.*' What does this tell you about Father Antonio's feelings when he heard the viola? Give **two** answers. [2]	
Answer: *Award one mark for each answer similar to:* First he thought it was terrible,; It gave him pain,; It made him wince. Then he thought it was funny,; He laughed about it/at her.	
Content domain reference	2g
Comprehension strategies	Identifying/explaining how meaning is enhanced by choice of words and phrases; Summarising
❓ '"*Everyone's the same,*"' What does father Antonio mean when he says this? Explain in detail. [2]	
Answer: *Award two marks for answers similar to:* She is not the only person who makes a horrible noise with an instrument.; He is trying to make her feel better (about her failure).	
Content domain reference	2d
Comprehension strategies	Making inferences

3 Look at the second section of the story. **Find** and **copy** a **group of words** that tells you that Father Antonio is thinking to himself about his choice of instrument. [1]	
Answer: pushed out his lower lip	
Content domain reference	2g
Comprehension strategies	Identifying/explaining how meaning is enhanced by choice of words and phrases; Making inferences
4 What does father Antonio think about the flute as a musical instrument? Tick **one** box. [1]	
Answer: The flute makes the loveliest music.	
Content domain reference	2b/d
Comprehension strategies	Making inferences; Retrieving and recording information
LEVEL: Deeper	
1 Which of the following is closest in meaning to *bestiary*, as it is used here. Tick **one** box. [1]	
Answer: a collection of animals	
Content domain reference	2a/2d
Comprehension strategies	Giving meaning of words in context; Making inferences
2 Why does Sister Cattina make her fingers into claws? [1]	
Answer: to mimic a lobster	
Content domain reference	2d
Comprehension strategies	Making connections; Making inferences
3 What is the difference between Father Antonio's reaction to Laura trying the viola, and his reaction to her trying the flute? Use evidence from the text to help you answer. [2]	
Answer: *Award one mark for each piece of evidence similar to:* He winced and thought her viola attempt was terrible.; It made him look like he was sucking a lemon.; Her attempt with the flute makes him speak slowly and thoughtfully.; He gives her lots of praise.; He says angels will listen to her if she practises.	
Content domain reference	2h
Comprehension strategies	Making comparisons within the text; Making inferences
4 What impression does this text give you of Father Antonio? Choose **one** description, then give evidence to support your choice. [3]	
Answer: *Award one mark for each piece of evidence similar to:* He loves music – He has a music room.; He appreciates good music.; He closed his eyes and smiled (and talks of angels). He is fun-loving – He laughed/he roared/he jokes about animals. He is a good teacher – He laughs/jokes about mistakes.; He says everyone's the same. *Accept any unique/reasonable answer.*	
Content domain reference	2d
Comprehension strategies	Making connections; Making inferences

Unit 7

Answers: Stargazing

	LEVEL: Towards
1 According to the text, what are stars made of? [1]	
Answer: very hot gas or plasma	
Content domain reference	2b
Comprehension strategies	Retrieving and recording information; Recall
2 Why are red dwarf stars less bright compared with other stars? Tick **one** box. [1]	
Answer: They are cooler.	
Content domain reference	2b
Comprehension strategies	Retrieving and recording information; Clarifying
3 Mark these facts about constellations as true or false. [2]	
Answer: True (given); True; False; False *Award one mark for two correct answers; two marks for three correct answers.*	
Content domain reference	2b/d
Comprehension strategies	Retrieving and recording information
4 Give **two** names for a well-known constellation that gets its name from Greek mythology. [2]	
Answer: Orion; The Hunter	
Content domain reference	2b
Comprehension strategies	Retrieving and recording information; Recall
	LEVEL: Securing
1 Place these stars in order of how fast they burn, from the fastest to slowest. [1]	
Answer: blue giant; yellow dwarf; red dwarf	
Content domain reference	2b
Comprehension strategies	Retrieving and recording information; Clarifying
2 Look at the table of stars and their descriptions. **Find** and **copy one** word that could be replaced with *blend* or *mixture*. [1]	
Answer: combination	
Content domain reference	2b
Comprehension strategies	Retrieving and recording information; Clarifying
3 Why might some stargazers argue with the idea of a brown dwarf being a type of star? Give **two** reasons. [2]	
Answer: It is dim whereas stars are bright.; It isn't big enough to be a star.	
Content domain reference	2b/d
Comprehension strategies	Retrieving and recording information; Making inferences
4 The following statements show the events that take place when a star dies. Number them 1-6 to show the correct sequence. [1]	
Answer: The stardust scatters. (5); It blows itself up. (3); It burns up all its fuel. (1) (given); A small spot forms. (4); New stars are formed. (6); It expands to a red giant. (2)	
Content domain reference	2b
Comprehension strategies	Retrieving and recording information

	LEVEL: Deeper
1 a) How are the names of constellations helpful? [1] b) What problem do people sometimes have with them? [1]	
Answer: a) They can help you recognise the patterns of the constellations /stars. b) It can be hard to see how some of them represent their name. *Award one mark for each section.*	
Content domain reference	2b
Comprehension strategies	Retrieving and recording information; Clarifying
2 Do stars twinkle? Answer the question using evidence from the text. [1]	
Answer: *Award a mark for yes or no, as long as the explanation from the text is applied correctly. Examples of acceptable answers are:* Yes, because when the light hits the Earth's atmosphere it looks twinkly. No, but it looks like they do because when the light hits the atmosphere it looks like it twinkles.	
Content domain reference	2b
Comprehension strategies	Retrieving and recording information; Clarifying
3 a) What is unusual about the way in which the *Seven Sisters* cluster can be spotted? [2] b) Explain why this happens, according to the text. [1]	
Answer: a) *Award up to two marks for:* They are easier to spot if you don't look at the stars.; When you look at them, they seem to disappear.; You can only see them from the corner of your eye if you look to the side of them. b) *Award one additional mark for:* The nerve cells in the centre of your eye cannot pick up the faint light, only the nerve cells at the corner can.	
Content domain reference	2b
Comprehension strategies	Retrieving and recording information; Clarifying
4 Which of the following would make the best replacement title for this text? Tick **one** box. [1]	
Answer: Stars and Constellations	
Content domain reference	2c
Comprehension strategies	Summarising; Making connections

Unit 8 — Answers: Alice's Adventures in Wonderland

LEVEL: Towards	
❓ Why has the author used *like the wind!* to describe how Alice moved? [1]	
Answer: *Award one mark for answers related to speed similar to:* to show that she was running very fast/at speed/very quickly/in a hurry	
Content domain reference	2g
Comprehension strategies	Identifying/explaining how meaning is enhanced by choice of words and phrases
❓ What is Alice worrying about as she falls down the tunnel? [1]	
Answer: *Award one mark for answers similar to:* her cat/Dinah; that her cat might go hungry	
Content domain reference	2b
Comprehension strategies	Retrieving and recording information; Clarifying
❓ Why was Alice feeling sad at this point in the story? Mark each statement as true or false. [2]	
Answer: True (given); True; False; False *Award one mark for two correct answers; two marks for three correct answers.*	
Content domain reference	2d
Comprehension strategies	Making inferences
❓ Number these events from the story 1–6 in the correct order. [2]	
Answer: Alice finds a key. (6); Alice falls down a hole. (1) (given); Alice lands on sticks and leaves. (4); Alice starts to fall asleep. (3); Alice sees the rabbit again. (5); Alice takes an empty jar of marmalade. (2) *Award one mark for three or four correct answers; two marks for all five correct.*	
Content domain reference	2c
Comprehension strategies	Summarising; Making inferences
LEVEL: Securing	
❓ Why does Alice start talking to herself? Give **two** reasons. [2]	
Answer: *Award one mark for each answer similar to:* There was nothing else to do as she was falling.; She was falling for a long time.; She was worrying about her cat.; She was wondering about things and there was no one else there at the time.	
Content domain reference	2d
Comprehension strategies	Retrieving and recording information; Recall; Making inferences
❓ '… the White Rabbit was hurrying' How else do you know that the rabbit is in a rush? Give **two** ways. [2]	
Answer: He says how late it's getting!.; Alice had to move fast to try to catch up with him.	
Content domain reference	2d
Comprehension strategies	Making inferences; Retrieving and recording information

Unit 8

3 When the rabbit disappears around the corner, Alice finds herself in a hall. Mark each statement about the hall as true or false. [2]	
Answer: False (given); True; True; False; True *Award one mark for two or three correct answers; two marks for all four correct.*	
Content domain reference	2b
Comprehension strategies	Retrieving and recording information; Clarifying
4 **Find** and **copy** the **group of words** to show Alice's feeling of relief when the key fits. [1]	
Answer: to her great delight	
Content domain reference	2a
Comprehension strategies	Giving meaning of words in context
LEVEL: Deeper	
1 How can you tell that Alice is falling for a long time? Give **three** ways. [3]	
Answer: 'Either the well was very deep or she fell slowly'.; She had plenty of time as she went down.; She had nothing else to do - which suggests she had time. *Accept any unique/reasonable answer.*	
Content domain reference	2d
Comprehension strategies	Making inferences; Retrieving and recording information
2 What type of story is *Alice in Wonderland*? Tick **one** box. [1]	
Answer: a fantasy	
Content domain reference	2c
Comprehension strategies	Summarising; Making connections
3 Apart from the talking rabbit, give **three** other things that are very unusual about the story. [3]	
Answer: The rabbit hole turns into a well and then into a hall.; Alice comes across furniture and furnishings down a rabbit hole (lamp, table, curtains).; The well is walled with bookshelves, a cupboard and even marmalade.; the small size of things in the hall e.g. table, doors and key. *Accept any unique/reasonable answer.*	
Content domain reference	2c
Comprehension strategies	Summarising; Making connections
4 From her actions, thoughts and words in the text, which words would best describe Alice's personality? Circle **two** words and explain your answers with evidence from the text. [3]	
Answer: *Accept two of the following:* thoughtful, brave, curious (*one mark*) Thoughtful: She thinks about her cat.; She doesn't just drop the marmalade jar, but puts it away into a cupboard. Brave: She doesn't show any fear when she's falling in the darkness or when she can't seem to find a way out.; She looks down as she's falling. Curious: She wonders about things e.g. how many miles she's been falling.; She follows the rabbit through the rabbit hole and keeps following. *Award a further two marks for reasons supported by evidence.* ***Do not accept:*** *selfish or cowardly.*	
Content domain reference	2d
Comprehension strategies	Making connections; Making inferences

© Pearson Education Limited 2018   *Pinpoint English Comprehension Year 4*   119

Unit 9

Answers: Taking the Shot

LEVEL: Towards	
❶ Number these events from the story 1–5 in the correct order. [1]	
Answer: He kicks the ball as hard as he can. (2); The coach high-fives him. (5); The goalie catches the ball. (3); He sees a clear line to the net. (1) (given); The whistle blows. (4); *Award one mark for three correct answers; two marks for all four correct.*	
Content domain reference	2c
Comprehension strategies	Summarising; Clarifying
❷ Look at the third paragraph. Why was it particularly important to win this match? [1]	
Answer: The winner would go through to the county championships.	
Content domain reference	2b
Comprehension strategies	Retrieving and recording information; Clarifying
❸ **Find** and **copy** the **group of words** that tell you that he spots the clear line all of a sudden. [1]	
Answer: in an instant	
Content domain reference	2a
Comprehension strategies	Giving meaning of words in context; Identifying/explaining how meaning is enhanced by choice of words and phrases
❹ What is meant by *keep my cool* as it is used here? Mark each answer as true or false. [2]	
Answer: False (given); True; False; True *Award one mark for two correct answers; two marks for three correct answers.*	
Content domain reference	2d/2g
Comprehension strategies	Making inferences; Identifying/explaining how meaning is enhanced by choice of words and phrases
LEVEL: Securing	
❶ How do you know that the narrator and Alex are playing well together? Tick **one** box. [1]	
Answer: They were passing and making good progress.	
Content domain reference	2d
Comprehension strategies	Retrieving and recording information; Making inferences
❷ What was his *only hope*? [1]	
Answer: *Award one mark for answers similar to:* shooting quickly (because the goalie was a bit slow)	
Content domain reference	2d
Comprehension strategies	Making inferences; Making connections; Clarifying
❸ With which foot does the narrator take the shot? [1]	
Answer: his right foot	
Content domain reference	2d
Comprehension strategies	Making inferences; Clarifying

Unit 9

4 '… *my coach gave me a high-five … my team mates kept saying, "Nice try"'* What does this information tell you about the narrator's team? [1]	
Answer: *Award one mark for answers similar to:* They are kind.; They can tell he did his best.; They are trying to cheer him up.; They don't feel as bad as he does.	
Content domain reference	2g
Comprehension strategies	Identifying/explaining how meaning is enhanced through words and phrases; Making inferences
5 Look at the last paragraph. **Find** and **copy one** word that means *most important*. [1]	
Answer: crucial	
Content domain reference	2a
Comprehension strategies	Giving meaning of words in context
LEVEL: Deeper	
1 **Find** and **copy** the **group of words** that makes it seem as though the whistle was laughing at his failure. [1]	
Answer: The whistle blew its mocking sound.	
Content domain reference	2a
Comprehension strategies	Giving meaning of words in context; Making inferences
2 What is different about the first paragraph compared with the rest of the story? Finish both of these sentences. [2]	
Answer: *Award marks for answers similar to:* a) how he feels about matches that depend on/come down to the last few seconds; matches that make him tense b) one particular match; the last minute of the match last weekend *Award one mark for a) and one for b).*	
Content domain reference	2h
Comprehension strategies	Making comparisons within the text; Summarising
3 How does the author feel in the second paragraph? How do you know? How does he feel in the last paragraph? How do you know? [3]	
Answer: second paragraph: anxious; worried; tense; He can't stand it because he hates matches that come down to the last few seconds, and he is playing in one. last paragraph: disappointed; devasted; terrible because he feels that the loss of the match was all his fault.; He really wanted to win (the important match) and they lost, due to him. *Award one mark for suggesting how the author feels in each paragraph. Award two marks for suggesting how he feels and adding one explanation. Award three marks for suggesting how he feels and two explanations.*	
Content domain reference	2h
Comprehension strategies	Making inferences; Clarifying; Making comparisons within the text
4 Which of the following would work best as a replacement title for *Taking the Shot*? [1]	
Answer: My Biggest Disappointment	
Content domain reference	2c
Comprehension strategies	Making inferences; Summarising

Unit 10

Answers: I Like to Stay Up

	LEVEL: Towards
1 Number these events of the poem 1-5 to put them in the right order. [1]	
Answer: She covers herself up. (5); She jumps into bed. (4); She gets sent to bed. (2); She listens to some ghost stories. (1) (given); She feels scared. (3) *Award one mark for three correct answers; two marks for all four correct.*	
Content domain reference	2c
Comprehension strategies	Retrieving and recording information; Summarising; Making inferences
2 What does *tingly* mean here? Tick **one** box. [1]	
Answer: thrilled	
Content domain reference	2a
Comprehension strategies	Giving meaning of words in context
3 Which line of the poem tells you that she makes sure that the bedclothes cover her up completely? [1]	
Answer: From me feet to me head.	
Content domain reference	2
Comprehension strategies	Retrieving and recording information; Making inferences
4 'Then is when I does wish I read Me book instead' *Instead* of doing what? Explain what she is wishing, and why. [2]	
Answer: *Award one mark for the answer and one for the explanation:* She wishes she had read her book instead of listening to jumbie/ghost/scary stories because then she wouldn't be scared.; Now she is scared (and she wishes she wasn't).	
Content domain reference	2b/2d
Comprehension strategies	Making inferences; Making connections
	LEVEL: Securing
1 Look at the first verse. How does she experience the ghost stories? Tick **one** box. [1]	
Answer: Adults are telling them.	
Content domain reference	2b
Comprehension strategies	Retrieving and recording information; Clarifying
2 What word could you use here that is similar in meaning to *dread*? [1]	
Answer: fear/terror/worry/anxiety	
Content domain reference	2a
Comprehension strategies	Giving meaning of words in context
3 Why might she call the jumbie stories *stupid*? Mark these explanations as true or false. [2]	
Answer: False (given); False; False; True *Award one mark for two correct answers; two marks for three correct answers.*	
Content domain reference	2d
Comprehension strategies	Making inferences; Empathising

6 Draw lines to match the short descriptions of some of the verses to the verse number. [2]	
Answer: dread (4) (given); wishes she didn't listen (7) (given); sent to bed (3); listening (1); excited (2) *Award one mark for two correct answers; two marks for three correct.*	
Content domain reference	2c
Comprehension strategies	Making inferences; Summarising
LEVEL: Deeper	
7 a) At what point does she change from enjoying the exciting jumbie stories, to being scared? [1] b) Why does this happen? [2]	
Answer: a) *Award one mark for:* It happens when she is sent to bed by her mother. b) *Award two additional marks for a thorough explanation similar to:* They were exciting when she was with everyone/with all the grown-ups, but she becomes frightened when she goes to her bed and is alone.	
Content domain reference	2d
Comprehension strategies	Making inferences; Making connections; Clarifying
8 Why do you think the poem is written in the first person (using *I*) rather than third person (using *she*)? [2]	
Answer: *Award two marks for answers similar to:* The reader feels close to her feelings.; You feel as if you are with her.; You feel like you are also experiencing what she's going through. *Accept any unique/reasonable answer.*	
Content domain reference	2g
Comprehension strategies	Identifying/explaining how meaning is enhanced by choice of words and phrases; Making inferences
9 Which of the below would work as a replacement title for *I Like to Stay Up*? [1]	
Answer: From Fun to Fear	
Content domain reference	2c
Comprehension strategies	Summarising; Evaluating; Making inferences

Unit 11

Answers: My Dad's a Birdman

LEVEL: Towards	
1 Number these events from the story 1-4 in the correct order. [1]	
Answer: Lizzie makes sure her father eats some toast. (3); Lizzie wakes her father up. (2); Lizzie prepares breakfast. (1); Lizzie's father says he's going to fly. (4) *Award one mark for two or thrree correct answers; two marks for all four correct.*	
Content domain reference	2c
Comprehension strategies	Summarising; Clarifying
2 Mark these statements about Lizzie as true or false? [2]	
Answer: False (given); True; True; False *Award one mark for two correct answers; two marks for three correct answers.*	
Content domain reference	2b/d
Comprehension strategies	Retrieving and recording information; Making inferences; Clarifying
3 Why does Lizzie start counting? [2]	
Answer: *Award two marks for answers similar to:* to hurry him out of bed; to scare or threaten him to get up; to give him a time limit; She is going to punish him/do something nasty if he doesn't get up.	
Content domain reference	2d
Comprehension strategies	Making inferences; Clarifying
4 What does *nibbled* tell you about the way he ate? [1]	
Answer: He took small/tiny bites.	
Content domain reference	2a
Comprehension strategies	Giving meaning of words in context; Clarifying
LEVEL: Securing	
1 **Find** and **copy one** word that shows that dad was *unsteady* coming down the stairs. [1]	
Answer: stumbled	
Content domain reference	2a
Comprehension strategies	Giving meaning of words in context; Retrieving and recording information
2 *'Then she smoothed his hair down and brushed it. She straightened the collar of his pyjama jacket.'* What **two** things does this sentence suggest about Lizzie's relationship with her dad? [2]	
Answer: *Award one mark for each answer similar to:* She cares for him/is his carer.; She's like a parent/mum.; She wants him to be smart.	
Content domain reference	2d
Comprehension strategies	Making inferences; Empathising
3 What does Lizzie mean when she says: *"You can't go on the way you are."* Mark each answer as true or false. [2]	
Answer: False (given); True; True; False *Award one mark for two correct answers; two marks for three correct answers.*	
Content domain reference	2b
Comprehension strategies	Making inferences; Clarifying

❹ 'Lizzie rolled her eyes' What do these words suggest that Lizzie is thinking about her dad's statement? Tick **one** box. [1]	
Answer: Oh, no. Here we go again!	
Content domain reference	2g
Comprehension strategies	Identifying/explaining how meaning is enhanced by choice of words and phrases; Making inferences
LEVEL: Deeper	
❶ Why might the author have used the word *ordinary* in this opening sentence? Give **two** reasons. [2]	
Answer: *Award one mark for each answer similar to:* This is what Lizzie does every morning.; It's a normal morning for Lizzie.; It makes the rest of the events (getting her dad up and feeding him) more of a surprise, because that's not very ordinary (for most people).	
Content domain reference	2g
Comprehension strategies	Identifying/explaining how meaning is enhanced by choice of words and phrases; Summarising
❷ What **two** things do you learn about Lizzie's character from the description of her getting up and getting ready? Give evidence from the text. [2]	
Answer: *Award one mark for each thing you learn about Lizzie's character, with relevant evidence, up to two marks:* She gets up quickly/doesn't lie in bed.; She keeps herself clean/tidy.; She is able to make breakfast. *Accept any unique/reasonable answer.*	
Content domain reference	2d
Comprehension strategies	Summarising; Making inferences
❸ Lizzie: 'scrubbed behind her ears … put on her uniform …' Dad: 'his hair all wild and his face all hairy' What might the author be suggesting about each of the characters, from these **two** pieces of evidence? [2]	
Answer: *Award one mark for each answer similar to:* Lizzie: looks after herself/keeps clean/smart; takes responsibility for herself Dad: does not look after himself OR: Lizzie and her dad are opposites - one is very clean/smart/responsible/sensible, the other is scruffy/messy/lazy/not sensible.	
Content domain reference	2h
Comprehension strategies	Making comparisons; Making inferences

Unit 12

Answers: The Merry Adventures of Robin Hood

LEVEL: Towards	
❶ How long did Robin Hood stay hidden in the woods? [1]	
Answer: one year	
Content domain reference	2b
Comprehension strategies	Retrieving and recording information; Recall
❷ Look at the fourth paragraph. How did the Sheriff of Nottingham congratulate himself? Tick **one** box. [1]	
Answer: with a slap on the leg	
Content domain reference	2b
Comprehension strategies	Retrieving and recording information; Clarifying
❸ Which of the below best matches the meaning of *bold* as it is used here? Tick **one** box. [1]	
Answer: brave	
Content domain reference	2a
Comprehension strategies	Giving meaning of words in context; Identifying/explaining how meaning is enhanced by choice of words and phrases; Clarifying
❹ Draw lines to match the characters to the facts about them. [2]	
Answer: Robin Hood – leads the outlaws. (given) the Merry Men – choose Robin to lead them. the Sheriff – wants to capture Robin. poor families – receive food from Robin. men of the town – laugh about catching the outlaw. *Award one mark for two or three correct answers; two marks for all four correct.*	
Content domain reference	2b
Comprehension strategies	Retrieving and recording information; Summarising; Clarifying
LEVEL: Securing	
❶ What does the word *too* tell you about the men joining Robin Hood at this point in the story? Tick **one** box. [1]	
Answer: They had been treated in the same way as Robin.	
Content domain reference	2a
Comprehension strategies	Giving meaning of words in context; Identifying/explaining how meaning is enhanced by choice of words and phrases
❷ According to the text, when did Robin Hood and his men give money and food to the poor families? [1]	
Answer: in times of need	
Content domain reference	2b
Comprehension strategies	Retrieving and recording information; Clarifying
❸ Why did Robin Hood and his men think it was all right to steal from the rich? [1]	
Answer: *Award one mark for answers similar to:* They were stealing from rich men the money they had taken from the poor.	
Content domain reference	2d
Comprehension strategies	Retrieving and recording information; Making inferences

Unit 12

🖉 What was the Sheriff's second plan? Mark each explanation as true or false. [2]	
Answer: True (given); False; True; False	
Award one mark for two correct answers; two marks for three correct answers.	
Content domain reference	2b
Comprehension strategies	Retrieving and recording information; Recall; Clarifying
LEVEL: Deeper	
🖉 According to the first paragraph, how were the Merry Men similar *to* Robin Hood? Tick **two** boxes. [2]	
Answer: They had been outlawed.; They lived in the woods.	
Content domain reference	2d
Comprehension strategies	Retrieving and recording information; Making inferences
🖉 Why might the Sheriff think that his second plan would get Robin Hood to come into the town? [3]	
Answer: *Award one mark for each answer similar to:* He knew that the gold arrow would tempt Robin to enter the competition.; He knew that Robin was good at archery/would want to enter an archery competition/would think he could win an archery competition.; He spread news of the competition far and wide.	
Content domain reference	2f
Comprehension strategies	Making connections; Making inferences; Clarifying
🖉 **Find** and **copy one sentence** in the second paragraph that tells you the people trusted Robin Hood like he was a friend. [1]	
Answer: They felt he was one of them.	
Content domain reference	2g
Comprehension strategies	Identifying/explaining how meaning is enhanced by choice of words and phrases; Making inferences; Clarifying
🖉 How did the people of Nottingham show they respected Robin Hood? Mark each answer as true or false by ticking the correct box. [1]	
Answer: True; True; False; False	
Award one mark for two or three correct answers; two marks for all four correct.	
Content domain reference	2d
Comprehension strategies	Making inferences; Empathising

© Pearson Education Limited 2018   Pinpoint English Comprehension Year 4   **127**

Unit 13

Answers: Natural Measures

LEVEL: Towards	
❶ What examples of *natural measures* are given in the first paragraph? [2]	
Answer: parts of the body; seeds; stones *Award one mark for two; two marks for all three.*	
Content domain reference	2b
Comprehension strategies	Retrieving and recording information; Recall
❷ What is the section headed *Measuring volume* about? Mark each answer as true or false. [2]	
Answer: True (given); False; True; False *Award one mark for two correct answers; two marks for three correct answers.*	
Content domain reference	2b/c
Comprehension strategies	Retrieving and recording information; Summarising
❸ What was the price of the *Pink Star*? Tick **one** box. [1]	
Answer: £53.7 million	
Content domain reference	2b
Comprehension strategies	Retrieving and recording information; Recall
❹ Which of the following is closest in meaning to *container* as it is used here? Tick **one** box. [1]	
Answer: holder	
Content domain reference	2a
Comprehension strategies	Retrieving and recording information; Recall
LEVEL: Securing	
❶ Why is the text called *Natural Measures*? [1]	
Answer: *Award one mark for answers similar to:* It is about the way natural things (seeds and hands) were used to measure things.	
Content domain reference	2f
Comprehension strategies	Making connections; Making inferences; Clarifying
❷ What have all the measures in the table got in common with each other? [1]	
Answer: They are all body parts.	
Content domain reference	2b
Comprehension strategies	Retrieving and recording information; Clarifying
❸ Look at the section headed *Measuring weight*. Why was it important that many goods were weighed? Tick **one** box. [1]	
Answer: The weight gave the price.	
Content domain reference	2b
Comprehension strategies	Retrieving and recording information; Clarifying

Unit 13

🖉 What are the **three** main things you can learn from the table? [3]	
Answer: *Award one mark for each answer similar to:* to see (names of) some natural measures; to see what body part they used; to see what natural measures are used for; to see how long natural measures are in cm; the information in the column headings	
Content domain reference	2f
Comprehension strategies	Retrieving and recording information; Making comparisons within the text; Making connections
🖉 Look at the section headed *Making measurements match*. Why did the Egyptians make a standard cubit stick? [1]	
Answer: *Award one mark for answers similar to:* Everyone could measure things in the same way.; It made measuring more accurate.	
Content domain reference	2b/d
Comprehension strategies	Retrieving and recording information; Making inferences; Clarifying
LEVEL: Deeper	
🖉 Look at the section headed *Modern equivalent*. Which of the following is closest in meaning to *modern equivalent* as it is used in the table? Tick **one** box. [1]	
Answer: the same amount today	
Content domain reference	2a
Comprehension strategies	Giving meaning of words in context; Making inferences
🖉 Why do you think a sundial is a better way to tell the time than looking at the position of the sun in the sky? [2]	
Answer: *Award one mark for each answer similar to:* Looking at the sun is less accurate.; The sundial has numbers so you know the time.	
Content domain reference	2b
Comprehension strategies	Retrieving and recording information; Clarifying
🖉 Look at the section headed *Making measurements match*. a) What was really helpful about natural measures? [1] b) What was the big problem with natural measures? [1]	
Answer: a) easy to use b) not always accurate *Award one mark for each section.*	
Content domain reference	2b
Comprehension strategies	Retrieving and recording information; Clarifying
🖉 According to the text, why did people start to agree on using the same measures? [1]	
Answer: *Award one mark for answers similar to:* so they could trade with each other	
Content domain reference	2b/d
Comprehension strategies	Retrieving and recording information; Making connections; Making inferences

Unit 14

Answers: My Lemonade Stand

LEVEL: Towards	
❶ Look at *Day 1*. Why was the writer bored? [1]	
Answer: 'nothing I had to do'; 'nothing I wanted to do' *Must have both parts to award mark.*	
Content domain reference	2b
Comprehension strategies	Retrieving and recording information; Clarifying
❷ Look at *Day 2*. Mark these explanations of the problem as true or false. [2]	
Answer: False (given); False; True; False; True *Award one mark for two or three correct answers; two marks for all four correct.*	
Content domain reference	2b/d
Comprehension strategies	Retrieving and recording information; Making connections; Making inferences
❸ When did Dad sell lemonade? [1]	
Answer: when he was a boy	
Content domain reference	2b
Comprehension strategies	Retrieving and recording information
❹ Look at *Day 4*. **Find** and **copy** the **group of words** that tells you the blueberry lemonade was *extremely popular*. [1]	
Answer: very big hit	
Content domain reference	2f
Comprehension strategies	Identifying/explaining how meaning is enhanced by choice of words and phrases; Making inferences
LEVEL: Securing	
❶ What was the *missile*? [1]	
Answer: a lemon/a piece of yellow fruit	
Content domain reference	2d/2a
Comprehension strategies	Making inferences; Giving meaning of words in context
❷ Look at *Day 1*. Give **two** pieces of evidence that show you Dad was in a good mood. [2]	
Answer: *Award one mark for each answer*: He tells a joke.; He chuckles.	
Content domain reference	2b
Comprehension strategies	Retrieving and recording information; Clarifying
❸ Look at *Day 1*. **Find** and **copy one** word that tells you the writer thought the idea of fresh lemonade was *delightful*. [1]	
Answer: appealing	
Content domain reference	2a
Comprehension strategies	Retrieving and recording information; Making inferences
❹ What was a *bore*? Mark each answer as true or false. [2]	
Answer: True (given); False; False; True *Award one mark for two correct answers; two marks for three correct answers.*	
Content domain reference	2d
Comprehension strategies	Retrieving and recording information; Making inferences

	LEVEL: Deeper
1 '… Dad's *feeble* attempt to cheer me' What is Dad's *feeble* attempt? [1]	
Answer:	Dad says the writer looks like they have been sucking lemons, so he throws them another lemon.
Content domain reference	2b/d
Comprehension strategies	Making inferences; Clarifying
2 In addition to *feeble* what word tells you that the writer does not think Dad's joke is funny? [1]	
Answer:	unamused
Content domain reference	2g
Comprehension strategies	Identifying/explaining how meaning is enhanced by choice of words and phrases; Making inferences; Clarifying
3 What evidence is there that Dad is a good problem solver? Give **three** examples from the text. [3]	
Answer:	*Award one mark for each answer similar to:* He made money for himself when he was a child by selling lemonade.; He suggests adding blueberries (in case people got fed up of normal lemonade).; He suggests making lollies (to preserve the lemonade).
Content domain reference	2f
Comprehension strategies	Making connections; Making inferences; Clarifying
4 Look at *Day 5*. a) Why can't the writer sell blueberry lemonade on Day 5? [1] b) Why is this a disaster? [1]	
Answer:	a) No one wants the lemonade on a miserable wet day.; There are no customers due to bad weather. b) They have spent all the money on lemonade no one wants.; They have invested a lot of time, and effort as well as money, making the stall beautiful. *Award one mark for each section.*
Content domain reference	2d
Comprehension strategies	Making inferences; Empathising

Unit 15

Answers: Sleeping for Survival

	LEVEL: Towards
❶ According to the text, what is hibernation? [1]	
Answer: a long rest in winter months; a deep sleep for several months.	
Content domain reference	2b
Comprehension strategies	Retrieving and recording information; Recall
❷ Give **two** reasons why some animals hibernate. [2]	
Answer: *Award one mark for each answer similar to:* It helps them survive the coldest time of the year.; It saves energy in the winter.; It is hard to find food.; Food is scarce in the winter.	
Content domain reference	2b
Comprehension strategies	Retrieving and recording information; Clarifying
❸ Draw lines to match the animals to their hibernation and aestivation behaviours. [2]	
Answer: bats – 4-6 months, in caves (given) hedgehogs – up to 6 months in a cold winter ladybirds – 5-6 months, huddled together frogs – aestivate if really hot, under logs *Award one mark for two correct answers; two marks for three correct answers.*	
Content domain reference	2b
Comprehension strategies	Retrieving and recording information; Making connections; Clarifying
❹ **Find** and **copy one** word very near the end of the text that means *toughest*. [1]	
Answer: harshest	
Content domain reference	2a
Comprehension strategies	Giving meaning of words in context; Clarifying
❺ Circle the names of the animals in this list which hibernate. [1]	
Answer: bats; hedgehogs; ladybirds	
Content domain reference	2b
Comprehension strategies	Retrieving and recording information
	LEVEL: Securing
❶ What happens to the body of an animal during hibernation? Give **three** examples. [3]	
Answer: *Award one mark for each answer similar to:* heart rate slows; breathing slows; body temperature drops; does not eat/take in more food; does not make waste	
Content domain reference	2b
Comprehension strategies	Retrieving and recording information; Clarifying
❷ In very hot countries, why do frogs need to aestivate? [2]	
Answer: *Award one mark for each answer similar to:* They are cold-blooded which means they can't cool themselves enough to survive in the heat.; There is little or no water.	
Content domain reference	2b
Comprehension strategies	Retrieving and recording information; Clarifying

3 Which of these problems might stop a hedgehog from surviving the winter? Mark each problem as true or false. [2]	
Answer: False (given); False; True; False *Award one mark for two correct answers; two marks for three correct answers.*	
Content domain reference	2b
Comprehension strategies	Retrieving and recording information; Clarifying
4 Circle the word in the list below that is closest in meaning to *signals*, as it is used here. [1]	
Answer: shows	
Content domain reference	2a
Comprehension strategies	Giving meaning of words in context; Clarifying
LEVEL: Deeper	
1 What does *scarce* tell you about the food? Tick **one** box. [1]	
Answer: There is not much food.	
Content domain reference	2a
Comprehension strategies	Giving meaning of words in context; Clarifying
2 What purposes does this text have? Give **two** reasons. [2]	
Answer: *Award one mark for each answer similar to:* It gives information about hibernation.; It tells you how to help hibernating animals in certain situations. [1]	
Content domain reference	2h
Comprehension strategies	Making comparisons within the text; Clarifying
3 a) What is the difference between hibernation and aestivation? [1] b) What are the similarities? [1]	
Answer: a) Hibernation is in winter (when there is little or no food) and aestivation is in summer (when there is little or no water). b) Both are long sleeps.; Both help animals survive tough weather/harsh conditions. *Award one mark for each section.*	
Content domain reference	2b
Comprehension strategies	Summarising; Clarifying
4 Why is it a bad idea for a ladybird to hibernate in a house? [2]	
Answer: *Award one mark for each answer similar to:* The warmth of the house wakes them up (makes them think it is spring).; There is not any food for them to eat because it is still winter.	
Content domain reference	2b
Comprehension strategies	Clarifying; Retrieving and recording information
5 Why is this text called *Sleeping for Survival*? [1]	
Answer: It is about staying alive/avoiding death by sleeping.	
Content domain reference	2c
Comprehension strategies	Summarising; Making connections

Unit 16

Answers: The Secret Garden

LEVEL: Towards	
1 At the beginning of the extract, what is Mary not used to? Tick **one** box. [1]	
Answer: liking people	
Content domain reference	2b
Comprehension strategies	Retrieving and recording information; Clarifying
2 Mark each description of the robin as true or false. [2]	
Answer: False (given); True; False; True *Award one mark for two correct answers; two marks for three correct answers.*	
Content domain reference	2b/d
Comprehension strategies	Retrieving and recording information; Making inferences; Clarifying
3 Number these main events 1-6 to put in this extract. Put them in the correct order. [1]	
Answer: Mary talks to the robin. (3); Mary sees a doorknob. (6); Mary hears the robin. (2); Mary walks next to a wall. (1) (given); The robin hops over a pile of earth. (4); Mary finds a key. (5)	
Content domain reference	2c
Comprehension strategies	Making inferences; Summarising
4 Find and copy two separate words that are bird noises. [2]	
Answer: chirp(ed); twitter(ed)	
Content domain reference	2a
Comprehension strategies	Giving meaning of words in context; Clarifying
LEVEL: Securing	
1 'Mary had begun to like the garden, and she had begun to like the robin.' What does this tell you about how Mary used to feel? [1]	
Answer: *Award one mark for answers similar to:* She didn't like the garden or the robin before – she has just begun to.	
Content domain reference	2f
Comprehension strategies	Making inferences; Identifying/explaining how meaning is enhanced by choice of words and phrases
2 What does *peeped* tell you about the **trees**? Tick **one** box. [1]	
Answer: They are only a bit taller than the wall.	
Content domain reference	2a
Comprehension strategies	Giving meaning of words in context; Retrieving and recording information
3 'It looked like it had been buried for a long time.' What is *it*? How does it look like it had been buried for a long time? [2]	
Answer: *Award one mark for each answer:* It is a key.; It is rusty.	
Content domain reference	2b/d
Comprehension strategies	Retrieving and recording information; Making inferences

Unit 16

✏ What was the *most interesting thing*? Tick **one** box. [1]	
Answer: finding the key and the door	
Content domain reference	2d
Comprehension strategies	Making inferences; Clarifying
LEVEL: Deeper	
✏ How do we know that Mary was unfriendly once? [2]	
Answer: *Award one mark for each answer similar to:* She was not used to liking people.; She forgot that she had ever been unfriendly.	
Content domain reference	2d
Comprehension strategies	Making inferences; Making connections
✏ **Find** and **copy a group of words** that tell you Mary is *incredibly happy*. [1]	
Answer: She didn't even want to breathe.	
Content domain reference	2g
Comprehension strategies	Identifying/explaining how meaning is enhanced by choice of words and phrases
✏ '"Maybe it has been buried for ten years,"' Mary said in a whisper. Mark each explanation of why she might be whispering as true or false. Tick the correct box. [2]	
Answer: True; True; False; False *Award one mark for two or three correct answers; two marks for all four correct.*	
Content domain reference	2d
Comprehension strategies	Summarising; Making inferences
✏ 'She always said that what happened next was magic.' What happened, and why did she think it was magical? [2]	
Answer: *Award one mark for each answer similar to:* One gust of wind was strong enough to show her the door knob just after she had found the key.	
Content domain reference	2d
Comprehension strategies	Making inferences; Clarifying
✏ What led Mary to find the key? [2]	
Answer: *Award one mark for each answer similar to:* A dog had dug a hole (looking for a mole) and this dug up the key.; The robin hopped over the earth and that led Mary to see it.	
Content domain reference	2f
Comprehension strategies	Making connections; Making inferences

Unit 17 — Answers: Who Has Seen the Wind? / Hurt No Living Thing

LEVEL: Towards	
1 Look at *Who Has Seen the Wind?* Mark each description of the poem as true or false. [2]	
Answer: True (given); False; True; False *Award one mark for two correct answers; two marks for three correct answers.*	
Content domain reference	2c
Comprehension strategies	Retrieving and recording information; Summarising; Clarifying
2 **Find** and **copy a** word that means *shaking*. [1]	
Answer: trembling	
Content domain reference	2a
Comprehension strategies	Giving meaning of words in context
3 Look at *Hurt No Living Thing*. Draw a line to match the creature to its description. [1]	
Answer: *Award one mark for all correct answers:* gnat – dancing grasshopper – light of leap cricket (given) – chirping cheerily worms – harmless moth – dusty wing beetle – fat	
Content domain reference	2b
Comprehension strategies	Retrieving and recording information
LEVEL: Securing	
1 In *Who Has Seen the Wind?* how does the strength of the wind differ in the first and second verses. Give evidence for your answers. [2]	
Answer: Verse 1: softer wind – makes the leaves tremble *(award one mark)* Verse 2: stronger wind – makes trees bow *(award one mark)*	
Content domain reference	2d
Comprehension strategies	Retrieving and recording information; Making inferences
2 Why has the poet chosen to write only about very small creatures in *Hurt No Living Thing*? Mark each explanation as true or false. [2]	
Answer: True (given); True; False; False *Award one mark for two correct answers; two marks for three correct answers.*	
Content domain reference	2f
Comprehension strategies	Making inferences; Clarifying; Making connections
3 Look at *Hurt No Living Thing*. **Find** and **copy one** word that is closest in meaning to *happily*. [1]	
Answer: cheerily	
Content domain reference	2a
Comprehension strategies	Giving meaning of words in context; Clarifying

Unit 17

4 Look at *Hurt No Living Thing*. Why might the poet have chosen to describe the creatures' details? Tick **two** boxes. [2]	
Answer: To show they all have different characteristics.; To make you notice their special qualities. *Award one mark for one correct; two marks for both correct.*	
Content domain reference	2f
Comprehension strategies	Making inferences; Clarifying; Making connections
LEVEL: Deeper	
1 In *Who Has Seen the Wind?* what is the effect of the repetition in the first two lines of each verse? Tick **one** box. [1]	
Answer: It emphasises that no one sees the wind.	
Content domain reference	2d
Comprehension strategies	Clarifying; Making inferences
2 Look at *Hurt No Living Thing*. What is the effect of listing little living things? [2]	
Answer: *Award one mark for each answer similar to:* There are lots of things that could be hurt.; It makes you think you shouldn't hurt anything.; It makes you realise there are many creatures, all living in their own way.; The 'harmless' at the end makes you realise they are all harmless.	
Content domain reference	2c
Comprehension strategies	Summarising; Identifying/explaining how meaning is enhanced by choice of words and phrases; Making comparisons within the text
3 Find and **copy** the **group of words** that describes how an animal jumps. [1]	
Answer: so light of leap	
Content domain reference	2g
Comprehension strategies	Identifying/explaining how meaning is enhanced by choice of words and phrases; Making inferences
5 What do the two poems tell you about the poet? [2]	
Answer: *Award one mark for each answer similar to:* She likes nature.; She notices details.; She sees things that not everyone would see. ***Do not accept:*** *answers that refer to a single poem, e.g. She likes small creatures,; She wants to protect living things.*	
Content domain reference	2h
Comprehension strategies	Making comparisons within the text; Making inferences

Unit 18

Answers: Mount Everest

LEVEL: Towards	
❶ What is the name of the mountain range in which Mount Everest is found? [1]	
Answer: the Himalayas	
Content domain reference	2b
Comprehension strategies	Retrieving and recording information; Recall
❷ List the three tallest mountains after Mount Everest. [3]	
Answer: K2; Kangchenjunga; Lhotse *Award one mark for each correct answer, up to three marks.*	
Content domain reference	2b
Comprehension strategies	Retrieving and recording information; Clarifying
❸ Mark each fact about Mount Everest as true or false. [2]	
Answer: False (given); True; False; True; False *Award one mark for two or three correct answers; two marks for all four correct.*	
Content domain reference	2b
Comprehension strategies	Retrieving and recording information; Clarifying
❹ Sir Edmund Hillary reached the top of Mount Everest in 1955. Why is this important and remembered? Tick **one** box. [1]	
Answer: He was the first person to reach the summit.	
Content domain reference	2b
Comprehension strategies	Retrieving and recording information; Recall
LEVEL: Securing	
❶ Find **one** difficulty mentioned in the text that makes climbing Mount Everest not an easy task. [1]	
Answer: There is not much oxygen.	
Content domain reference	2d
Comprehension strategies	Making connections; Making inferences; Clarifying
❷ Look at the table. Why have these mountains been chosen to go into the table? [1]	
Answer: They are the ten tallest mountains in the world.	
Content domain reference	2d
Comprehension strategies	Retrieving and recording information; Making inferences; Making connections
❸ Which of the definitions below is closest in meaning to *adjust* as it is used here? Tick **one** box. [1]	
Answer: get used to	
Content domain reference	2a
Comprehension strategies	Giving meaning of words in context; Clarifying
❹ Find **two** things that climbers do at camps on Mount Everest. [2]	
Answer: *Award one mark for each answer similar to:* rest; prepare their supplies; let their bodies adjust (to altitude)	
Content domain reference	2b
Comprehension strategies	Retrieving and recording information; Making connections

Unit 18

5 'The summit of Mount Everest is covered in dazzling, deep snow all year round.' Explain why *sunglasses* are included in the list of special gear to protect climbers. [1]	
Answer: to protect their eyes from the dazzling snow	
Content domain reference	2d
Comprehension strategies	Making connections; Making inferences; Clarifying
LEVEL: Deeper	
1 Which of the following is closest in meaning to *an amazing feat* as it is used in this sentence? Tick **one** box. [1]	
Answer: an achievement that requires great courage, skill and strength	
Content domain reference	2a
Comprehension strategies	Giving meaning of words in context; Making inferences
2 'More than 250 people have died while climbing the mountain.' Why is this information included in the text? [2]	
Answer: *Award one mark for each answer similar to:* It is a very dangerous thing to do.; It shows the dangers of climbing Mount Everest.; It makes you realise that not everyone can climb it.; It adds sadness to the feeling of excitement/wonder.	
Content domain reference	2b/2d
Comprehension strategies	Retrieving and recording information; Making inferences; Clarifying
3 Look at the section headed *Sherpas*. a) Give **two** reasons why Sherpas make such excellent guides for visitors and climbers. [2] b) How else do Sherpas help climbers? [1]	
Answer: a) know Mount Everest well; famous for climbing skills b) transport things (on yaks)	
Content domain reference	2b
Comprehension strategies	Retrieving and recording information; Clarifying

Unit 19

Answers: Making Room for Bikes

LEVEL: Towards	
❓ Number the events of the incident 1-5 in order. [2]	
Answer: They slammed on the brakes. (3); The driver continued his journey. (5); They were enjoying a pleasant bicycle ride home. (1) (given); The sister fell off her bike. (4); A large vehicle pulled out in front of them. (2) *Award one mark for three correct answers; two marks for four correct.*	
Content domain reference	2b
Comprehension strategies	Retrieving and recording information; Clarifying
❓ Who was the letter-writer with when the incident happened? [1]	
Answer: his mum and (younger) sister	
Content domain reference	2b
Comprehension strategies	Retrieving and recording information; Clarifying
❓ Give **two** things the letter-writer says he and his family were doing to cycle safely. [2]	
Answer: *Award one mark for each answer similar to:* riding on the left; wearing hi-visibility jackets; wearing helmets; reflective lights on bikes	
Content domain reference	2b
Comprehension strategies	Retrieving and recording information; Recall
❓ Mark each fact about where the accident happened as true or false. [2]	
Answer: True (given); False; True; True *Award one mark for two correct answers; two marks for three correct answers.*	
Content domain reference	2b/d
Comprehension strategies	Retrieving and recording information; Making inferences
LEVEL: Securing	
❓ What is the serious problem affecting the town, according to the letter-writer? Tick **one** box. [1]	
Answer: There are no safe spaces for people to ride bikes.	
Content domain reference	2d
Comprehension strategies	Retrieving and recording information; Making inferences
❓ a) Find **two** things the letter-writer says other towns have done to improve cycling safety? [2] b) What additional safety suggestion does the letter-writer make? [1]	
Answer: a) cycle paths; cycle lanes; signs to warn drivers *Award two marks for each correct answer.* b) reducing speed from 30 to 20 mph *(award one mark)*	
Content domain reference	2b
Comprehension strategies	Retrieving and recording information; Clarifying
❓ **Find** and **copy one** word that tells you that the Parker family had to use their bicycle brakes very *quickly* and *powerfully*. [1]	
Answer: slam	
Content domain reference	2a
Comprehension strategies	Giving meaning of words in context; Making inferences

© Pearson Education Limited 2018 — Pinpoint English Comprehension Year 4

a) Who is the letter-writer writing to? [1] b) As well as his family, who is he writing the letter for? [1]	
Answer: a) the Mayor 　　　　　b) cyclists riding in the area (of Great Wittledon).	
Content domain reference	2c
Comprehension strategies	Summarising; Clarifying
LEVEL: Deeper	
Which of the following is closest in meaning to *brought to my attention*? Tick **one** box. [1]	
Answer: I have noticed it.	
Content domain reference	2f
Comprehension strategies	Making inferences; Clarifying
What clues are there that the Parker family had good brakes on their bicycles? [2]	
Answer: We were forced to slam on our brakes.; Had we not been able to stop so quickly. 　*Award one mark for the second piece of evidence; two marks for both pieces of evidence.* 　**Do not award marks:** *for the first statement alone.*	
Content domain reference	2d
Comprehension strategies	Making connections; Making inferences
'… can you really put a price on someone's head?' Why does the letter-writer say this? [2]	
Answer: *Award two marks for each answer similar to:* 　He knows the cost will be high, but not as bad as someone losing their life.; 　It will be expensive, but that is better than someone dying.	
Content domain reference	2f
Comprehension strategies	Making connections; Making inferences
What is the purpose of Josh's letter to the Mayor? [3]	
Answer: *Award one mark for each answer similar to:* 　It lets the Mayor know about the problem – that there are no safe spaces for people to ride bicycles in their town.; He wants to say he is worried someone may have an accident. 　*Accept any unique/reasonable answer.*	
Content domain reference	2c/h
Comprehension strategies	Summarising; Making inferences; Making connections ; Making comparisons within the text

© Pearson Education Limited 2018　　　Pinpoint English Comprehension Year 4

Unit 20

Answers: The Lion's Share

	LEVEL: Towards	
1 How many animals went hunting together? [1]		
Answer: four		
Content domain reference	2b	
Comprehension strategies	Retrieving and recording information; Recall	
2 Number the events of the incident 1-5 in order. [1]		
Answer: The animals agree to work together. (2); The animals feel hungry. (1) (given); The fox, jackal and wolf grumble and walk off. (5); They catch deer in the late afternoon. (3); The lion explains why he should get three portions. (4)		
Content domain reference	2c	
Comprehension strategies	Summarising; Making inferences	
3 What does *finally* tell you about their hunt? [1]		
Answer: It took a long time.		
Content domain reference	2a	
Comprehension strategies	Giving meaning of words in context; Clarification	
4 How is the appearance of the lion described? [1]		
Answer: eyes of gold; fur of velvet; claws of steel		
Content domain reference	2b	
Comprehension strategies	Retrieving and recording information; Clarifying	
	LEVEL: Securing	
1 Why were the animals hunting together? Give **two** reasons. [2]		
Answer: They were all hungry.; They realised that they had more chance of a meal if they worked together.; They were less likely to find food on their own.		
Content domain reference	2b	
Comprehension strategies	Retrieving and recording information; Recall	
2 '*The others mumbled something, but it could not be heard.*' Why do you think they did not argue with the lion? [1]		
Answer: They were too frightened to complain aloud.		
Content domain reference	2d	
Comprehension strategies	Making inferences	
3 **Find** and **copy one** word which has a similar meaning to *prize*. [1]		
Answer: reward		
Content domain reference	2a	
Comprehension strategies	Giving meaning of words in context; Clarifying	
4 Which of the following would make the best replacement title for the story? Tick **one** box. [1]		
Answer: The Selfish King		
Content domain reference	2c	
Comprehension strategies	Summarising; Making inferences	

Unit 20

	LEVEL: Deeper
1	a) Whose idea was it to divide the deer into four parts? [1] b) Why did the other animals *nod in agreement* at first? [1]
Answer:	a) the lion's b) They were happy for the lion to have a share and thought they would get their fair share too. *Award one mark for each section.*
Content domain reference	2d
Comprehension strategies	Retrieving and recording information; Making inferences
2	What does *unflinchingly* suggest about the way that the lion stared? Tick **one** box. [1]
Answer:	without any fear
Content domain reference	2g
Comprehension strategies	Identifying/explaining how meaning is enhanced by choice of words and phrases; Making inferences; Clarifying
3	Describe the personality of the lion as fully as you can, drawing on what he says and does. Give at least **two** pieces of evidence. [3]
Answer:	*Award up to three marks for two distinct answers similar to:* He is selfish and unfair because he doesn't share the food equally even though all the animals have worked together.; He is self-important because all his reasons are about his land, his household and his success. *Accept any unique/reasonable answer.*
Content domain reference	2f
Comprehension strategies	Making connections; Making inferences; Clarifying
4	Do you think the other animals will hunt with the lion again? Explain your answer based on your understanding of the text. Complete the sentences below. [1]
Answer:	No, because they will now know that he would never be fair.; No, because they would be unsafe if they tried to face up to/challenge him next time. *Accept any unique/reasonable answer.* **Do not accept:** any answers to yes.
Content domain reference	2e
Comprehension strategies	Visualising; Making inferences

This page is intentionally blank